SDT-1

SELF-DEFENSE TRAINING: LEVEL ONE

SELF-DEFENSE TRAINING: LEVEL ONE

SIMPLE TECHNIQUES AND STRATEGIES FOR PROTECTING YOURSELF AGAINST INTERPERSONAL HUMAN AGGRESSION

DERWIN J. BRADLEY

AuthorHouse™ LLC
1663 Liberty Drive
Bloomington, IN 47403
www.authorhouse.com
Phone: 1-800-839-8640

Published by AuthorHouse 07/08/2013

ISBN: 978-1-4817-7121-4 (sc)
ISBN: 978-1-4817-7122-1 (e)

Library of Congress Control Number: 2013912113

CONTENTS

SECTION I – LEGAL ISSUES 1

SECTION II – THE ART OF CONVERSATION 3

SECTION III – THE FIRST LINE OF DEFENSE 6

SECTION IV – STANCES AND BASIC MOVEMENTS 13

SECTION V – BLOCKS 19

SECTION VI – STRIKES, PUNCHES, AND KICKS 29

SECTION VII – SPECIALIZED STRIKES 56

SECTION VIII – ESCAPES/FALLS/GROUND DEFENSE 61

SECTION IX – COMBINATIONS DRILLS 74

SECTION X – REPORT WRITING 79

SECTION XI – BULLYING 83

SECTION XII – ANATOMY AND FORCE CONTINUUM CHART 86

SECTION XIII – DOMESTIC VIOLENCE 89

SECTION XIV – CRIMES 92

SECTION XV – CRIMINALS 98

SECTION XVI – WEAPONS OF CHOICE 103

SECTION XVII – ACTIVE COUNTERMEASURES! 106

SELF-DEFENSE TRAINING – LEVEL ONE

SIMPLE TECHNIQUES AND STRATEGIES FOR PROTECTING YOURSELF AGAINST INTERPERSONAL HUMAN AGGRESSION

This manual was written for use by College Students that are enrolled in Self-Defense courses provided by their respective Academic organizations. Collegiate Self-Defense courses are typically one semester long and the students learn a variety of basic techniques that will help them improve their personal safety abilities as well as their overall personal safety awareness. The techniques in this manual are explained in simple terms and some photographs are provided to help with training and practice sessions.

It should be noted that this manual can also be used by anyone who wants to improve their personal safety awareness and self-defense capabilities. It is recommended that each person attends a Basic Self-Defense Class with a qualified Instructor in conjunction with the use of this manual.

"Absorb what is useful,
Discard what is not,
Add what is uniquely
your own."

Bruce Lee

FOREWORD

> *"Karate is, and always has been a method of self-defense, never a technique of aggression. But it is much more than that. To the sincere student, it is a form of combined physical and mental discipline from which he can learn the value of personal attributes such as kindness and sincerity. To the karate master, self-control is quite as important as mastery of the various techniques."*
>
> *Sensei M. Nakayama*

My Martial Arts journey began when I was twelve years old. My father enrolled my brothers and me in a Judo class at the local community center. The Sensei was Japanese and taught only in Japanese so learning was painful and difficult. Luckily, his assistant, a young American man, was able to translate and save us from too much discomfort.

Judo was okay, but I grew up in the middle of several large neighborhoods and not all of the young men in those neighborhoods were what we would call "upstanding citizens", and fighting them required something more. I was kind of skinny and mild-mannered back then so the bully types often focused on me. Then, at age fourteen, I had a life-altering experience. I was hanging out with my younger brother and some friends at the local Junior High (Middle) School when an older kid began harassing us. I was the oldest and had to protect my younger brother so he focused on me. He beat me up pretty good for no reason.

Needless to say, I was furious! We told our big brother who reported later that he found that guy and thumped him for us. But that wasn't good enough for me. I swore that day that no one would ever do that to me again! I looked in the phone book and found a place called East Coast Martial Arts Supply. I had a part-time job cleaning schools after school so I took that money, hopped on my bicycle, and rode to the other side of town to the Martial Arts supply store and bought a book on Karate for Self-Defense.

It was summer time so I had plenty of time to practice. I spent at least four hours a day practicing techniques. I was leaving Junior High and starting High School so I wanted to be ready for the new challenge. My big brother had joined the Army that summer so I was now the oldest son at home. I had five sisters to look out for so I knew I would need some more training to deal with the thugs I would be attending high school with.

It turned out that I had a gift for the Arts and by the time school started I was quite skilled at self-defense. I had found a local Martial Arts instructor that taught me and several other boys for free in the elementary school playground, which really honed my skills. Later I trained with a Sensei in the Ketsu Rai system. After he moved away I found a USA GOJU Sensei who was also an Orlando Police Officer. I entered high school well-skilled and highly confident. I was challenged several times by the regular bullies and stood my ground, ready to defend myself. They all backed down without any violence occurring.

Since that memorable summer day I have studied many styles of Martial Arts including Kyokuskin and some Tang Soo Do, and have dedicated my life, training, and skills to protecting those who cannot protect themselves. My Martial Arts training has been the key to winning numerous violent confrontations in the line-of-duty. For you, Basic Self-Defense training can be the difference between a ride to the hospital, and filling out a police statement and going home.

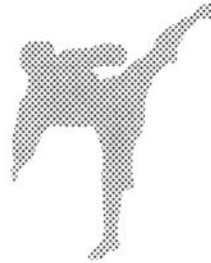

SECTION I – LEGAL ISSUES

"Hey baby, there ain't no easy way out! Hey now, I stand my ground; and I won't back down!"

-TOM PETTY AND THE HEARTBREAKERS

SELF DEFENSE

Self-defense—Protection of oneself, one's family or one's property from harm by others. The right to such protection can be a valid defense to a criminal prosecution. An individual who is attacked, or whose property is threatened by another, generally may defend himself using necessary force. The person acting in self-defense must not have incited the attacker, and there must be clear imminent peril to justify force. Criminal Law makes an important distinction between the use of Non-Deadly Force and Deadly Force. A victim may utilize Deadly Force, such as discharging a loaded gun, only when he/she believes that he/she will perish at the hands of the attacker or suffer serious bodily injury. However, the law does not excuse the use of Deadly Force against an unarmed assailant, unless there were mitigating circumstances, e.g., the presence of more than one attacker or the attacker's reputation for extreme violence. The victim must justifiably employ Non-Deadly Force in situations where he/she is threatened with injury, but not death. REF. *BLD, CBA, CL, DC, LTC*. Source; Dictionary of Crime

STAND YOUR GROUND LAW

A **stand-your-ground law** states that a person may justifiably use force in self-defense when there is reasonable belief of an unlawful threat, without an obligation to retreat first. The concept sometimes exists in statutory law and sometimes through common law precedents. One key personal assistant is whether the concept only applies to defending a home or vehicle, or whether it applies to all lawfully occupied locations.

Under these legal concepts, a person is justified in using deadly force in certain situations and the "stand your ground" law would be a defense or immunity to criminal charges and civil suit. The difference between immunity and a defense is that immunity bars suit, charges, detention and arrest. A defense, such as an affirmative defense, permits a plaintiff or the state to seek civil damages or a criminal conviction but may offer mitigating circumstances that justifies the accused's conduct.

More than half of the states in the United States have adopted the Castle doctrine, stating that a person has no duty to retreat when their home is attacked. Some states go a step further, removing the duty of retreat from other locations. "Stand Your Ground", "Line In The Sand" or "No Duty To Retreat" laws thus state that a person has no duty or other requirement to abandon a place in which he has a right to be, or to give up ground to an assailant. Under such laws, there is no duty to retreat from anywhere the defender may legally be.[1] Other restrictions may still exist; such as when in public, a person must be carrying firearms in a legal manner, whether concealed or openly.

"Stand your ground" governs U.S. federal case law in which right of self-defense is asserted against a charge of criminal homicide. The Supreme Court of the United States ruled in *Beard v. U.S.* (158 U.S. 550 (1895)) that a man who was "on his premises" when he came under attack and " . . . did not provoke the assault, and had at the time reasonable grounds to believe, and in good faith believed, that the deceased intended to take his life, or do him great bodily harm . . . was not obliged to retreat, nor to consider whether he could safely retreat, but was entitled to stand his ground."[2][3]

Justice Oliver Wendell Holmes, Jr. declared in *Brown v. United States* (256 U.S. 335, 343 (16 May 1921)), a case that upheld the "no duty to retreat" maxim, that "detached reflection cannot be demanded in the presence of an uplifted knife".[4] [Source: Internet].

VICARIOUS LIABILTY

vicarious liability n. sometimes called "imputed liability," attachment of responsibility to a person for harm or damages caused by another person in either a negligence lawsuit or criminal prosecution. Thus, an employer of an employee who injures someone through negligence while in the scope of employment (doing work for the employer) is vicariously liable for damages to the injured person. In most states a participant in a crime (like a hold-up) may be vicariously liable for murder if another member of the gang shoots and kills a shopkeeper or policeman. (See: liability)

In the case of self-defense training; the trainer or instructor is responsible for what he/she teaches or presents to the students. I taught Defensive Tactics at the Criminal Justice Institute Police Academy for twelve years. I took some time off from teaching for a few years to pursue other endeavors. When I returned to renew my Instructor's Certification, I asked the Instructor leading the Recruit class where they were in the State Standards book (for Defensive Tactics), he stated, "Oh, we don't use that anymore." He handed me a piece of paper with some techniques on it. I asked in disbelief, "So you don't teach State Standards here anymore?" He shook his head. I left and never returned. In Law Enforcement the stakes are just too high to not adhere to set policies and standards. I wasn't willing to risk being dragged into court because an officer used an off-the-wall, non-approved technique on a citizen and caused serious harm. Fortunately, you are not bound by such rigid standards, but you are still required to act responsibly when using force to defend yourself or your family. Some of the techniques in this manual can cause serious injury or even death. **THESE TECHNIQUES ARE NOT TO BE KNOWINGLY USED IN THE COMMISSION OF ANY CRIME OR CRIMINAL ACT.** You are instructed to use this training for ***SELF-DEFENSE ONLY.***

SECTION II – THE ART OF CONVERSATION

"It is more important to outthink your opponent than to outfight him"
-SUN TZU

THE ART OF TALKING YOUR WAY OUT A FIGHT (Police Officers call it Verbal Judo).

There may come a time where you will find yourself in a small room/space with a dangerous and unstable person and you have to do some serious smooth talking to avoid a violent confrontation. You will have to dig deep down inside of yourself for the inner strength and quiet calm you need to calm the beast that is threatening you. Allow me to share a story with you.

Many years ago I was on patrol when I received a call from headquarters to respond to home for a possible sexual assault on a young girl. When I arrived at the house I was met by a blonde woman who had a look of fear and concern on her face. As I entered the living room, I was met by the woman's husband, an African American man who was clearly enraged. He was about six feet tall, weighing in at about 200 pounds. He was in fact, a heavily muscled man. Clean-shaven, he was wearing a black t-shirt, green cut-off military pants, and black combat boots. He was pacing when I walked in and suddenly stopped and started at me.

"You can't stop me!" he snapped. He didn't wait for an answer. He just started pacing again.

I looked at his wife and asked her what happened. I learned that her sixteen year old daughter had spent the night at a friend's house and claimed to have been molested by a young man as they swam in the pool. The result was red marks on the daughter's neck.

The husband came back into the picture. "You can't stop me! I am going to find that boy and kill him and you can't stop me! I was in the Navy SEALs for seventeen years and you can't stop me!" He promptly went into the bedroom and brought out a box with military documents and medals to prove his claim.

I put my hands up, palms facing him and said, "Let's just calm down and let me talk to your daughter." I was hoping the gesture would show him that I was willing to talk and that I did not want any trouble.

The husband went off on another tirade, at which time I repositioned myself in the small living room and got as much distance and furniture between us as possible. I also quietly called for back-up on the radio.

I finally spoke to the daughter alone and found out that she had not been molested, and it was her boyfriend who met her at her friend's house and put hickies on her neck. She pinched herself and bruised her entire neck in order to cover her hickies. The husband/stepfather was shocked and apologized repeatedly.

Then, keeping true to the Special Ops type swagger, he smiled and asked, "What would you have done to try to stop me?"

I smiled and said, "I would drawn my pistol, shot you three or four times from the hip, then raised it up and put two between your eyes."

He was shocked. "Why would you do that?"

I explained that because he was a Navy SEAL and he was threatening to kill someone and challenged me to stop him, I could easily articulate in my report on why I had to shoot him dead. I never told him about my Martial Arts expertise or my military training. I didn't tell him that I had trained Special Forces soldiers in Hand to Hand combat. I wanted him to think that he had all the advantages, and I really didn't want to fight him in that small living room. So in this case, talking calmly and staying calm really paid off.

Years ago in the police profession someone coined the term "Verbal Judo", the art of talking calmly to a suspect in an attempt to avoid a physical confrontation. Some Police Officers quickly ridiculed it and poked fun at the term. But it simply makes sense to "smooth talk" someone when the odds don't appear to be in your favor; or when you just want to take the high road and avoid a violent confrontation. But remember; even as you try to talk your way out a fight, plan to win it if it comes down to that.

THE ARTFUL DODGER—Some years before the encounter with the Navy SEAL, I had an encounter with an Army Special Forces Soldier. I was working the midnight shift when the Watch Commander called me to a barricaded suspect scene. The suspect was a Green Beret, body builder, and a 5th Degree Black Belt who had battered his wife and was barricaded in the house. The house was completely dark and he was inside alone. The Watch Commander wanted to go in and get him. I advised against it. There was no way that I was going in there with this guy's background. They took my advice and decided to wait until morning. The next day, when he came out of the house, it took six officers just to handcuff him! Luckily he wasn't fighting or resisting with force! He later told us that he was waiting just behind the front door with a "Rambo" style knife and was going to kill as many of us as he could.

A QUICK WORD ABOUT ENCOUNTERS WITH EVIL

One of the biggest obstacles I have to overcome when teaching self-defense classes to civilians is that they simply cannot believe that anyone would want to hurt them or take from them. I was teaching a Women's Self-Defense class in a very upscale neighborhood and one the ladies said, "Well this is an upscale neighborhood. What if the bad guy is good-looking and wearing a suit?" The other women nodded in agreement, validating this question. I said, "Two words. Theodore Bundy. You know him right? Murdered and decapitated at least 12 victims. He kept some of the heads in his apartment. He was smart and handsome." The room always falls quiet as my response sinks in.

So I have to preface every class with a short speech on how the bad guy doesn't care if you're a good person, he doesn't care if you go to church every Sunday or feed the homeless on Wednesdays. He doesn't care that you work hard every day and attend PTA meetings. All he cares about is that you have something he wants and he is going to take it! No, you cannot always talk your way out of it. As a matter of fact, sometimes the more you beg, plead, or try to reason, the more you embolden or empower him. Some criminals feed off of your fear in some very disturbing ways. Of course it is ultimately your decision whether to try to talk your way out of a dangerous situation, submit to the will of the aggressor, or fight/resist with all of your might. This book was written for people who choose to fight with the goal and expectation of winning. Let's get started.

SECTION III – THE FIRST LINE OF DEFENSE

"Officer, I was just walking to my car in the parking lot and he came out of nowhere!"
-TYPICAL CRIME VICTIM

COLONEL COOPER'S AWARENESS COLOR CODE SYSTEM

The Color Code system was designed to give soldiers a basis and understanding of their awareness level and how it affects their response to potential threats or imminent danger. It will serve you very well in your effort to protect yourself from harm.

1. **WHITE**—You are unprepared and not ready to take defensive/offensive action. If you are attacked, you will probably never know what hit you.
2. **YELLOW**—You begin to understand that your life/safety is in danger and that you may have to take action.
3. **ORANGE**—You have indentified the threat/adversary and are prepared to take offensive/defensive action.
4. **RED**—You are in combat mode and will fight/shoot/take any action necessary to survive/win!!
5. **BLACK**—Your senses have overloaded and you shut down completely! You are of no use to yourself or the people who might have to depend on you. You will lose and/or die!

REMEMBER THE THREE D's OF SURVIVAL

1. **DETECT**! This is where your awareness comes in. Detect the threat and prepare for it!
2. **DENY**! Escape and evade if possible. Deny them access to you!!
3. **DESTROY!** You cannot escape/evade the threat. You must destroy/defeat them quickly or remove their ability to harm you.

WHITE is where most of you are in your daily activities.

YELLOW is where most Police Officers are when working. From there it can fluctuate through the entire spectrum in a matter of minutes several times a day.

RED is where the Aggressor works and lives. This is where you will have to meet him/her if you become his/her target.

SITUATIONAL AWARENESS

SITUATION \ siche' washen\ n 1. Location 2. Condition 3. job

AWARE \ e'waer\ adj : having realization or consciousness; aware-ness.

Most humans, particularly in today's high-tech society are so distracted that they are barely conscious of the world moving around them. Your gadgets distract you; your friends distract you; your children; and most of all, your thoughts REALLY distract you! So often in your daily routine your mind slips into auto-thought and you think and concentrate on everything in your life except the person that has been watching you since you walked into whatever public place you just arrived at.

The criminals know that you are distracted. In fact; they are counting on it because it makes their jobs that much easier. So many times I have been taking a report from a victim of a Robbery or Physical Assault and they said, "He came out of nowhere!" In reality, the criminal did not come out of nowhere. The more likely scenario was that the criminal was there the entire time, but you were not paying attention. Sometimes they do have really good hiding places, but if they can pick them out, so can you. So pay attention, notice who is noticing you, and be cautious of them.

That is where Situational Awareness comes into play. In the military and law enforcement we use that term to get the attention of soldiers and police officers to let them know to watch out for or be aware of certain events. For you it is the same. Take the definitions of both words literally and they mean having consciousness or realization of your condition and/or location.

For example; you are at the mall or supermarket. You are talking on the phone, texting, or otherwise pre-occupied as you enter the store and get right down to business. You didn't notice the man that came in right behind you and immediately began tracking you through the mall/store. You don't see him as he follows you from aisle to aisle and eventually back to your car or maybe even your home.

That is why before you out to work, shop, party, or even take out the trash; clear your mind a little and prep for the journey into that big old crazy world out there! We can teach you all the self-defense skills you need to protect yourself, but if you don't see the threat coming, it will do you no good. Wake up! The criminals are experts at human behavior and they know when you are NOT prepared or attentive!! Notice who is noticing you!

SITUATIONAL AWARENESS—What is my situation? Am I aware of my surroundings?

Several years ago I was in Atlanta attending a government Terrorism Training Course when I decided to walk to dinner to a restaurant not too far from the hotel. As fate would have it, that section of the street was nearly deserted and it was starting to get dark. As I walked, I noticed a man leaning against the wall of a closed business. His eyes seemed to light up when he saw me coming. I quickly scanned my surroundings to see if he had any associates flanking me. As I got closer, he half-smiled and came off of the wall. (Story continued on the next page . . .)

THREAT ASSESSMENT

THREAT \'thret\ n 1: Expressions of intention to harm 2: things that threatens

ASSESSMENT \e—ses-ment\ n 1: the act of assessing. 2: evaluation: estimation 3: judgement of the motives, capabilities, and characteristics of a present adversary.

Okay, so you are up on your Situational Awareness and you have noticed the person(s) that have been following you or have focused their attention on you. The very first question you should ask yourself is; What is the potential threat and how should I deal with it?

When responding to a call, whether it be a traffic accident or a robbery in-progress, I always run through scenarios (in my mind), of potential dangers. Then, when I arrive on the scene, I immediately began sizing up and analyzing everyone there. If there is an obviously aggressive person; I formulate a plan to subdue them. Sounds overly aggressive? Not at all. Being mentally prepared to confront violence with a plan is critical to good self-defense.

First, make eye contact with the person. That way he/she knows that you know that they are targeting you. Remember; despite all of our intelligence and education, we are still animals and if you show weakness by looking away or down, the criminal will take that as a cue to move in for the attack.

While you are looking at him/her, get a good head to toe description. Then, do a quick scan of the area to see if they have accomplices nearby. You will have to decide quickly what to do. Do you go back inside and tell a store employee? Can you make it to your car? Can you outrun or outfight the person? Are there multiple assailants? Do you display or deploy your personal defense weapons that you are carrying? Should you dial 911 now? Are you in danger?

If the person is trying to make conversation and/or get close to you, (such as a person asking for a handout), hold up your hand and ask, "What do you want?" It may sound callous, but you should NEVER let strangers get within six feet of you in those types of situations. If you must err, err on the side of caution!

Finally, you must quickly decide what the person can do to you to cause you harm and what you must do to prevent them from doing so. Your brain is a remarkable machine and will give you the answers to virtually any question you ask. So when you are confronted with a potential threat or adversary you can ask yourself some simple questions: 1. Am I in danger? 2. Who is my enemy? 3. What can he/she do to harm me? 4. How do I stop him/her? If you are focused and determined, your brain will give the answers you need to at the very least take defensive action.

THREAT ASSESSMENT—Identify the Threat; Analyze the Threat; Devise a Plan of Action. Keep the process simple. Many of you don't understand violence so you want to ask why someone would do that. As a young Army Protective Services Agent I didn't ponder why

Terrorists wanted to kill us. I kept three simple questions in mind: Who are our enemies? What can they do to us? How do we stop them? See how close they are to the questions you must ask? Let's keep moving.

(Story continued) I determined that the man standing in front of me on that deserted sidewalk was a threat. Since I was both taller and heavier than he was, I assessed that he was armed and had evil intentions; or he was simply just going to ask for a handout. Either way, I wasn't taking any chances . . . .

ESCAPE AND EVASION PLAN

ESCAPE \ is' kap\ vb 1: get away or get away from 2: flight or avoidance of something unpleasant

EVASION \ I' vazhen\ n : act or instance of evading (or avoiding)

You have followed the first two steps of personal defense but somehow you have found yourself in a potentially dangerous situation. You have identified the threat and have made an assessment of the potential harm or danger to you (and those with you). Now you have to ask yourself, **"How do I avoid or escape this situation?"**

You may find yourself in a deserted parking garage with a person or persons that have made it clear that they want to do you harm. Can you get back inside to get help? Can you make it to your car, get in, get it started, and drive away before they get to you? Can you run away and get to help before they catch you?

You might find yourself being followed while walking (or jogging) down the street or driving in your car. You should immediately get on the phone and call the police! Do not call your mother in another state, your best friend, or your significant other! Only the police can track you and get to you while you evade the assailant(s). **DAIL 911!**

If you are at home and you hear a window break or an estranged mate kicks in the door. Can you get out of house before they catch you? Do you barricade yourself in a room and dial 911? Do you jump out of window even though you are on the second floor?

You should always check for emergency exits in every building and commercial transport vehicle that you enter. If you are in a volatile relationship, you should always have an exit/ escape strategy. You should always know how to get out of your place of employment quickly just in case one of your co-workers, a client, or a co-worker's violent significant other shows up with mayhem on his/her mind!

When you see trouble brewing around you, or you find yourself in a situation just doesn't feel right; that's your God-given instincts kicking in! Listen to them! They will save your life! Look at the situation, assess the threat, and then quickly make your move to avoid or escape harm!

(Story continued) I ran my escape and evasion plan through my head. The road was at least six lanes across and I didn't want to turn my back on this guy. . . .

IMMEDIATE ACTION DRILLS

Immediate Action Drills are moves, techniques, and responses that you should mentally and physically practice/rehearse to save yourself or your loved ones lives. These drills are not always just for self-defense as they are highly effective in all types of dangerous situations.

Interpersonal Human Aggression as described by Lt Colonel David Grossman, is the act of one or a group of human beings attacking a one or a group of other human beings. It seems that it is in our nature to want to physically hurt and even kill each other despite our highly civilized status on this planet.

When soldiers, particularly Special Operations troops, and Law Enforcement Officials are trained to perform extreme tasks under extreme conditions such as reloading a firearm during a firefight, the trainers stress repeatedly the need for Immediate Action Drills. The three tenets of Immediate Action Drills for self-defense are Surprise, Speed, and Aggression.

Typically, the criminal will have planned his/her crime and maybe even rehearsed it before coming after you. Serial Killers, Rapists, Home Invasion Robbers, Domestic Batterers are all examples of criminals that plan their crimes. Therefore, you, the casual, law-abiding citizen must use your secret weapon when you are attacked.

SURPRISE—When you activate or deploy your defensive measures, the criminal should not see it coming. For instance, if you choose to use Chemical Spray (Mace), don't threaten the person with it. Take it out, conceal it, and then surprise them with a two-second burst to the face! If you should choose to fight hand to hand, don't jump into a fighting stance and announce that you are a trained fighter. Hide your method of attack/defense until the last possible moment, then strike!

SPEED—Once you find yourself in a situation that you can't talk your way out of and you can't run away from, you may decide to fight. Should you decide to fight, attack as quickly and precisely as humanly possible. Whatever you are going to do; do it with all of the speed that you can generate! Your goal is to catch the attacker off-guard and quickly finish the fight.

AGGRESSION—The criminal will already have their aggression tuned up, get yours going too! You should turn into the Tasmanian Devil on them because they had no business or right to put their hands on you! Make them regret ever coming near you! Hit! Kick! Bite! Stomp! Scratch! Hit them with anything that isn't bolted down! Fight, survive, and win by any means necessary!!

PRE-EMPTIVE SELF-DEFENSE—"She/He who strikes first usually wins"—Ernest Emerson (Paraphrase)—If you find yourself in a situation where an attack is eminent, and you can't escape and you just can't talk your way out of it; go ahead and launch an attack. Get the first strike in and try with everything you have to end the confrontation quickly!

(The story finale . . .) So I decided not to try to evade this guy and opted for direct confrontation. As he came off of the wall and blocked my path, I quickly swept my coat back and put my hand on my pistol and asked, "Can I help you?" I used all of the tenets listed above to take the upper hand in this potentially dangerous situation. No way was I going to walk past this guy and hope for the best. He threw his hands up and rather quickly departed the area! *NOTE* If I had not been armed, I would have chosen to evade by crossing the street or turning around and going in the opposite direction.

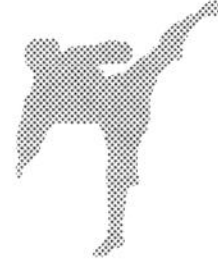

SECTION IV – STANCES AND BASIC MOVEMENTS

"Be firm yet not hard, soft yet not yielding"
-BRUCE LEE

BASIC READY STANCE—The next step in Self-Defense training is developing a good basic stance. In order to be able to block and absorb attacks, evade attacks, or counter attacks, you need to know how to stand and move. In this section, you will learn proper stance and movement for Basic Self-Defense.

You start by standing facing your adversary with your feet shoulder-width apart. If you are right handed, slide your right foot back a few inches (about a foot's length). If you are left-handed, bring your left foot back.

You knees should be slightly bent and your legs should be relaxed. Your weight should be evenly distributed on your feet. You should feel as though you can move quickly and easily in any direction.

Now, bring your hands up together in the "praying" position, about six inches from your chin. Drop your chin down into the "scolding" position (to protect the throat). Now, turn your hands so that your palms face out towards your adversary as if you were going to give a powerful shove. Your elbows are bent and stay close to the body to protect your ribcage. You are relaxed and breathing in through your nose, and out through your mouth.

This is the basic Ready Stance. Your feet are shoulder-width apart and off-set. Your hands are up and above your waste-line. Your palms are facing outward in the universal sign of "Hey, I am not a threat. Let's calm down. I don't want any problems." You should say it out loud and let everyone in the vicinity hear you. But in reality you are preparing to block, move, and strike if attacked.

Never face a threat with your hands down at your side! The moment that you know things are going bad, get your hands up and get into a good stance.

WAR STORY! When I was assigned to the Drug Enforcement Division's Uniformed Drug Unit, we had numerous physical confrontations (violent fights), every day. The Drug Dealers often violently resisted and some even wore spiked rings to try to severely injure us. We brought a new officer into the Unit who had a habit of talking to suspects with his hands in his pockets. We warned him several times but he did not listen. You guessed it! He got in a Drug Dealer's face one night and got his nose broken for his troubles! The Drug Dealer punched him square in the nose and bolted!! (We caught him rather quickly and took him into custody). The moral of the story is to keep your hands up!! Once you're sure you're going to have to fight, put your hands up so that you can block, deflect, and strike!!

FIGHTING STANCE—Same as the Ready Stance only your guard is up and you have your hands are balled into fists. This sends a clear message to the attacker that you are prepared to fight!

NOTE Many advanced/highly skilled fighters fight open-handed.

BASIC READY STANCE

Morgan is using an open-hand in her ready position. Matt is using closed fists indicating clearly that he is ready to fight.

LATERAL MOVEMENT

Proper Lateral movement is the difference between effectively and efficiently evading an attack, and stumbling over your feet, losing balance, and falling down! We will refer to the method of movement as Glide and Drag. You glide in the direction you want go, then drag the other foot along and immediately get back into the Ready Stance. Check yourself to make sure that you are back in a good Ready Stance.

Proper Lateral Movement is very simple. Get into your Basic Ready Stance. Clasp your hands together in front of you as you do this drill. This will help you get in the habit of keeping your hands up.

Glide and Drag Lateral movements help your move quickly and smoothly while maintaining a good stance and balance. They also help you detect obstacles in dark areas and prevent you from tripping over them.

Moving Forward: Glide forward with your lead foot, then drag the rear foot into proper position.

Moving Left: Glide to the left with your left foot, then drag your right foot into proper position.

Moving Right: Glide to the right with your right foot, then drag your left foot into proper position.

Moving Backwards: Glide to the rear with your rear foot, then drag your front foot into proper position. This technique is particularly important because you ***do not*** want to get caught stumbling backwards and off-balance during a fight. Once you start the backwards stumble, it is extremely difficult to regain your balance and the attacker will usually take advantage of that and knock you down.

OPENING THE DOOR

Opening the Door is circular movement used to evade someone or something that is charging straight at you. Typically, in this scenario the aggressor is trying to grab you or tackle you. Imagine yourself as a Matador evading an angry 1500 pound Bull with razor-sharp horns!

Open Left: From a Ready or Fighting stance. When the aggressor charges at you and gets close enough, you glide you left foot around behind you in an Arc, put your hands on the aggressor's upper body (shoulder area), and push him/her away as you turn with them. Turn and face them and be prepared for further aggression. *Note* The harder you push them, the more time it will take them to recover.

Open Right: From a Ready or Fighting stance. This time glide your right foot around behind you in an Arc and push/deflect the person away as you turn.

Always check your stance once you get back into position. Make sure your feet are shoulder-width apart. Point your toes forward. Flex your knees slightly. Don't lapse back into a lazy or off-balance stance because you might have to move quickly again! Stay on guard until you are safe!

Matt charges at Morgan.

Morgan moves to her left.

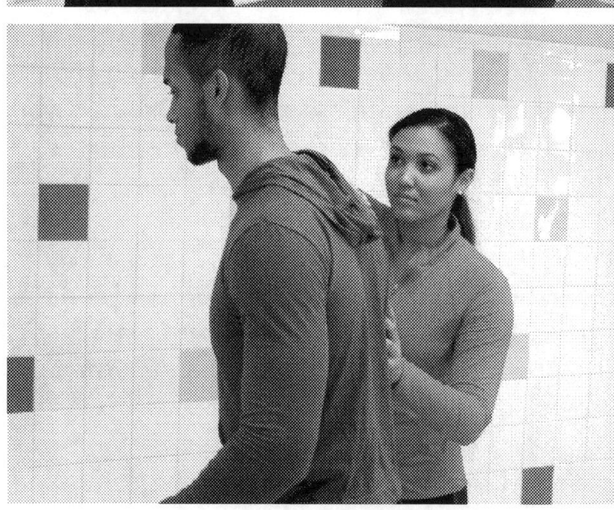

Morgan pushes Matt away.

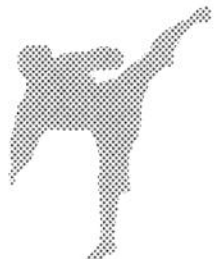

SECTION V – BLOCKS

"Shields up Scottie!"
-CAPTAIN JAMES T. KIRK,
USS ENTERPRISE-STAR TREK

To properly defend yourself, you must learn how to block and/evade an attack. If you can keep from getting hit, you can reduce your chances of getting hurt. Years ago, when Kickboxing became popular, several of my colleagues that had competed on the circuit came to me for fighting advice. They all had the same question; "How do I keep from taking such a beating?" After observing their fighting styles I noticed that they all had the same problem. They all focused on attacks and not enough on defense. In other words, they took a lot of unnecessary punishment just to try to land a punch or kick. I encourage you to develop a high degree of skill in blocking techniques. It will save you a lot of pain.

1. **HIGH BLOCK**—This block is intended to protect the head from an overhead strike or blow. (Typically by some type of weapon).
2. **SUPPORTED HIGH BLOCK**—Modified and supported version of the High Block.

Stand in the ready position. Typically, the hand in front (the lead hand) will do the initial blocking effort. Ideally, you want to be good enough to able to block on the side the attack is coming from. To perform the High Block, you raise your arm up so that your bicep is even with your ear. Your forearm should at a forty five degree angle above your head, with your palm facing the sky. This keeps the "meaty" side of your arm up so that it can absorb the impact of the attacker's arm or weapon. (Matt)

To make this a Supported High Block, take your other hand place it on your wrist or grab your wrist. You have now created a pyramid or "A frame" effect over your head. This block is ideal for smaller people who are defending themselves from a large opponent that is using an overhead attack. (Morgan).

You must remember to keep your knees flexed and have a good, wide base/stance so that you can absorb the impact of the blow/strike and not get knocked off-balance.

Morgan defends against an overhead, clubbing fist attack.

Morgan defends against an overhead knife attack.

MIDDLE BLOCK—Sometimes referred to as the **'OUTSIDE BLOCK'**. This block is intended to protect the head and face from attacks coming from the left or right.

SUPPORTED MIDDLE BLOCK—Modified and supported version the Middle Block.

Stand in the Ready Stance or Fighting Stance. Raise your lead hand so that your bicep is parallel to the ground and away from your body at a slight angle. Your forearm should be up so that your hand is level with your face and your palm is facing inward. The arm is basically an "L" shape next to your face that will block any attack from that side of the body.

The Supported Middle Block is designed for smaller people that are being attacked by a larger or more powerful person. Bring your blocking arm up into position. Bring your supporting arm up and either grab your wrist or place it against your wrist.

Remember to flex your knees and maintain a good wide stance so that you can absorb the force of the attack and not get knocked off balance. The force that the attacker is going to be coming at you with will probably knock you off balance if your feet are not properly planted!

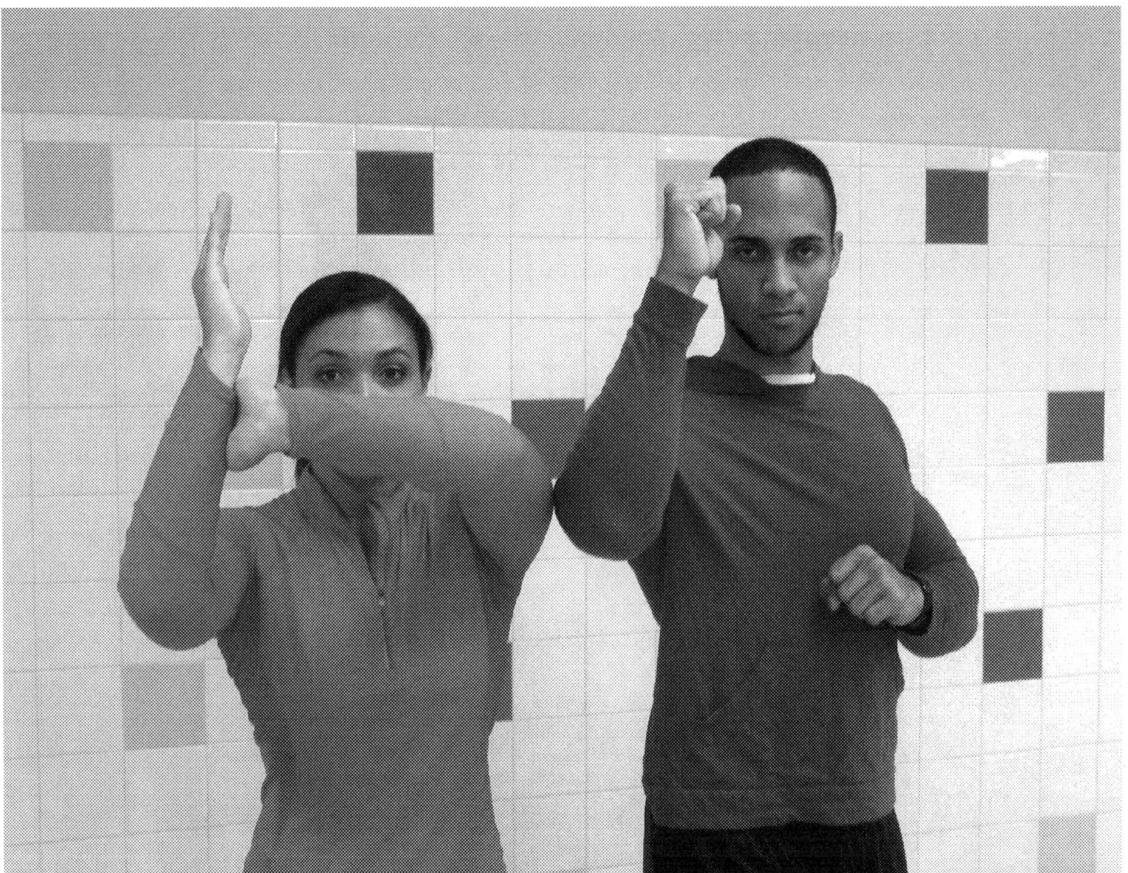

Morgan is using the supported Middle Block. Matt is using the standard Middle Block.

Morgan blocks a powerful attack from the left side.

DEFLECTION OR DEFLECTOR BLOCK—This block is intended to 'deflect' or redirect a punch, stab, or grab to the front of the body. This is a simple but very effective block that can be used to "deflect" nearly any frontal attack. From your Ready or Fighting Stance, use an open hand to push across your body as you deflect an attack.

Insure that you push the aggressor's arm hard enough that his/her attack is clearly and forcefully knocked away from you. Again also insure that you have a good, solid stance so that you can maintain good balance and deliver effective power.

Morgan is doing a standard Deflection Block while Matt is using the advanced version often used by skilled Martial Artists. Below: Morgan deflects an attempt to grab her.

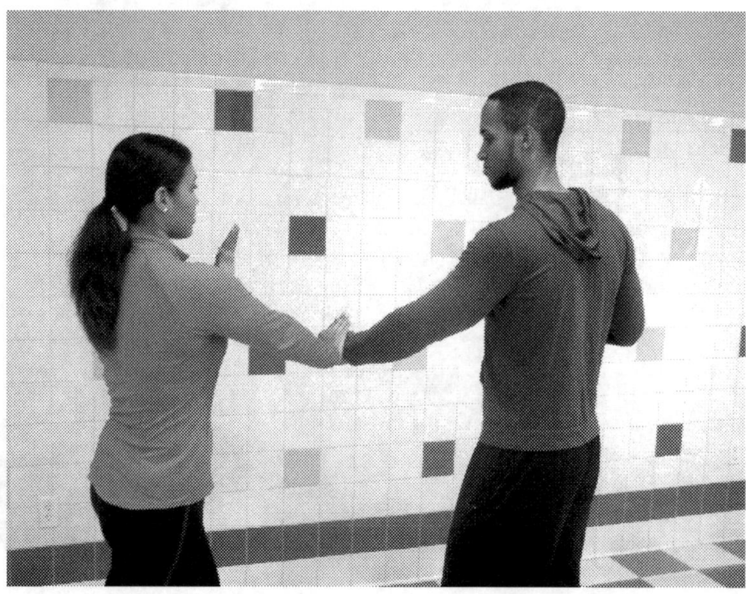

Above, Morgan deflects a knife attack.
Below, Matt deflects a punch with a modified Deflection Block.

LOW BLOCK—This block is intended to stop and/or deflect a kick to the groin area or lower extremities.

From your Fighting Stance (hands up with your fists closed), use your lead hand down in an Arc across the front of your body, stopping just at the outside of your thigh. Bring the arm back up immediately after deflecting the kick/attack. You should try to typically try to block with the arm on the side from where the attack is coming but it is not absolutely necessary.

You can also glide to the rear as you execute this block to increase your chance of effectively evading/blocking this attack.

Matt using a Low Block to deflect a kick aimed at his mid-section.

EMERGENCY BLOCK!—This block is intended to protect the face, head, and upper body from surprise and/or multiple strike attacks. The defender covers the face with his/her arms while using the elbows to stop incoming strikes. The intention is to try and get the attacker to injure his/her hands on the defender's elbows.

From the Ready or Fighting Stance, bring your fists up to your ears so that your elbows are pointed towards the aggressor. Lower your chin to your chest but keep your eyes on the aggressor. Your stance should be solid and powerful. (You can also use this technique if you are on your back).

Use the outside of your arms you block incoming attacks. Keep watching the aggressor's pattern and when you are ready, try to turn into the attack so that the aggressor hits the pointed edge of your elbows. You can also use your elbows to block uppercuts and knee strikes.

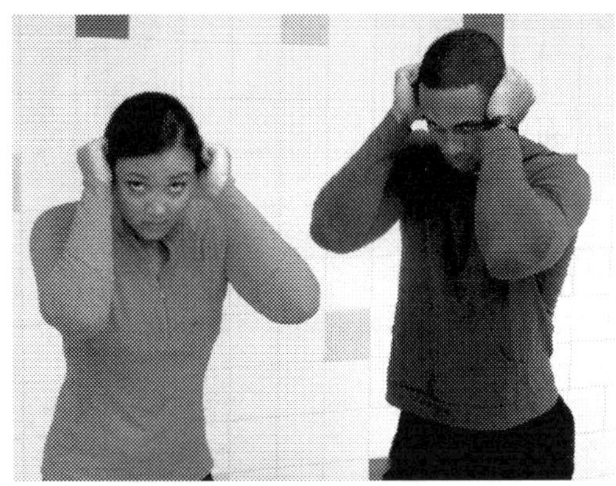

IRON WALL—This technique an extremely effective method of blocking kicking attacks and other types of attacks to the front of the body.

From the Ready or Fighting Stance, simply bring your knee up so that it is parallel to the ground. Drop your elbow to your knee, creating the "Iron Wall" effect. Immediately return to the Ready or Fighting Stance and prepare for more aggression.

Matt using the Iron Wall to defend against a front kick.

SECTION VI – STRIKES, PUNCHES, AND KICKS

"The less effort, the faster and more powerful you will be"
-BRUCE LEE

In the world of Soldiers and Law Enforcement Officials, the term 'Smooth is quick', is often used when performing tasks that require a lot of concentration and a high degree of skill. It is as true in self-defense as it is in shooting drills. I often repeat the words, 'relax, breath', numerous times during a training session. Tightly tensed muscles will burn precious energy that you will need to defend yourself. The more tense you are, the slower your response/reaction time will be. Try playing slap-tag with a cat. Notice how relaxed and unconcerned it appears as compared to the blinding speed it can generate when scratching your hand before you can withdraw it. The goal is to hit quickly and powerfully.

OPEN HAND PALM STRIKE-The Palm Strike is a very simple, but effective strike. I typically like to use it when I don't really want to hurt the person but I do want them know that I mean business. From your Ready/Fighting Stance, open your hand and strike the aggressor with the "heel" of your palm. That is the reason this strike is also referred to as the "Palm Heel Strike". Your aim point can be anywhere on the aggressor's body. Be sure to keep your fingers and thumb close together.

DOUBLE-TAP PALM STRIKE—This is a 1-2 type movement. You can strike left-right; or right-left. You can strike high-low, low-high, or in the same spot.

DOUBLE PALM STRIKE—Using both your hands; strike the aggressor's torso as hard as you can while step forward. Be sure to push off of the back foot.

Matt using a Double Palm Strike.

VERTICAL PUNCH—From the Fighting Stance, hold your fist vertically (instead of horizontally), and quickly strike the aggressor. Your aim point is typically soft tissue or soft parts of the body. Do not "load" your punch. "Loading" is when you draw your fist back before you punch. This will let the aggressor see your intentions and give him/her time to counter your moves.

DOUBLE-TAP VERTICAL PUNCH—This is a 1-2 strike used to attack multiple points on the aggressor's body. Example: The Left hand strikes to the face, the Right hand strikes to the body. (Remember to use your hips to generate power!).

DOUBLE VERTICAL PUNCH—Same as the Double Palm strike only you are using your fists.

Morgan demonstrates a single Vertical Punch and Matt demonstrates the Double Vertical Punch.

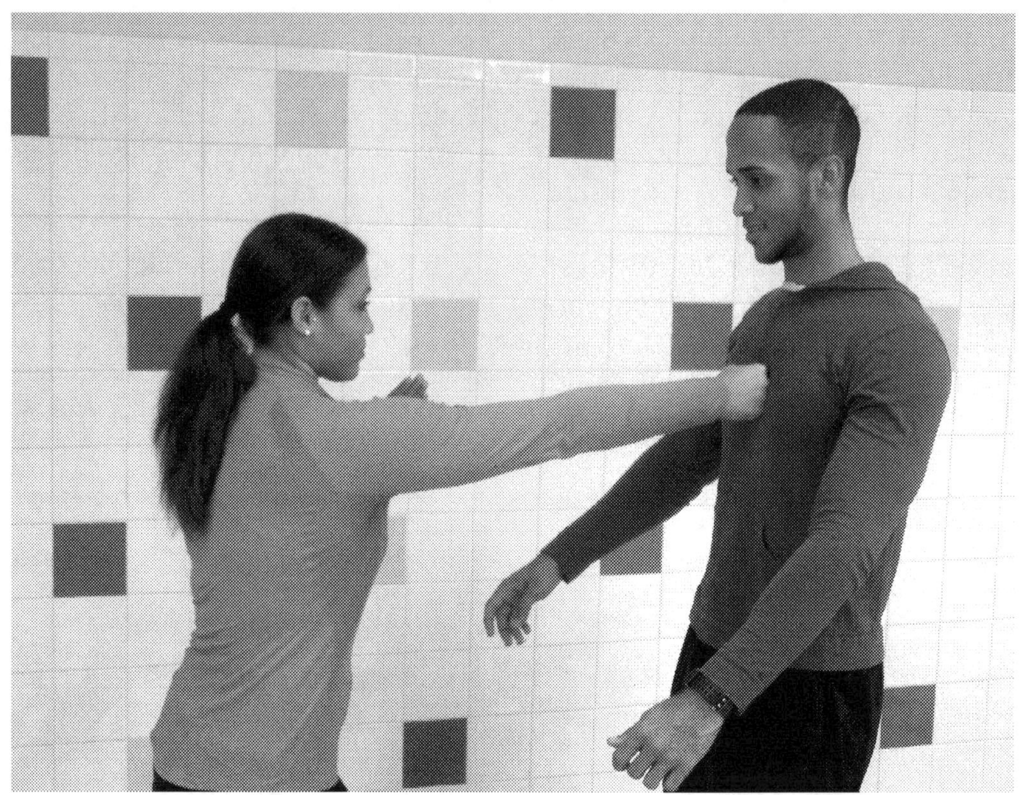

Morgan uses the Vertical Punch.

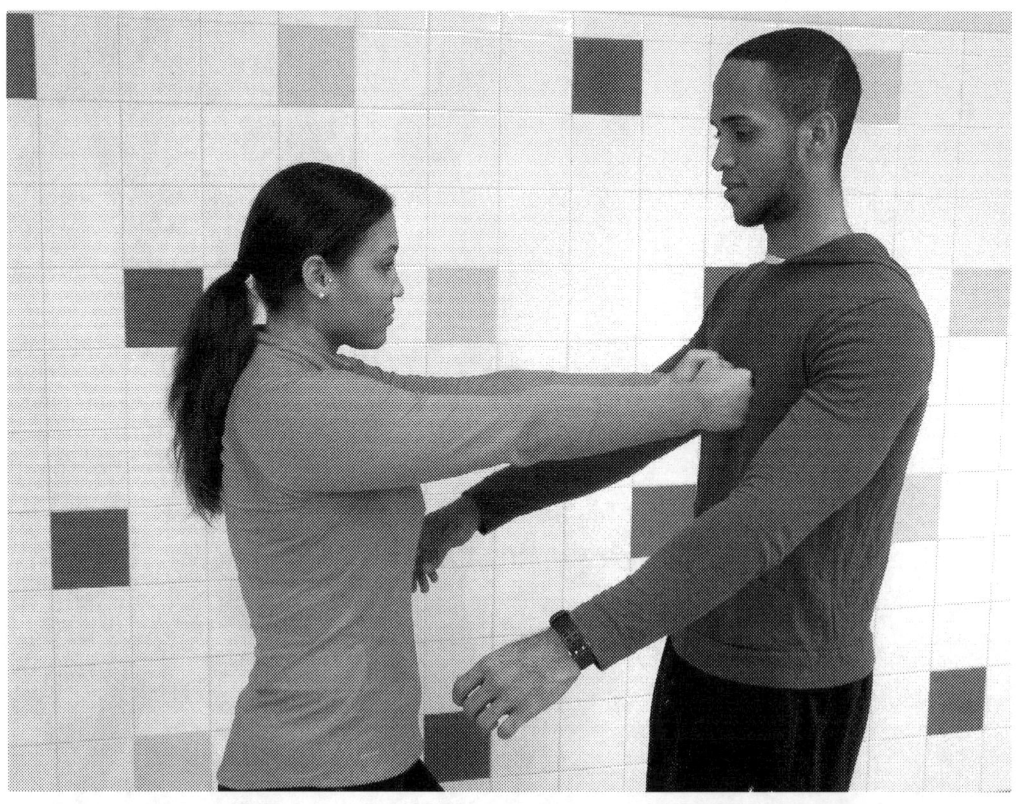

Double Vertical Punch—Remember to step forward to increase power.

Matt uses a modified version of the Double Vertical Punch called the "U" Punch.

HAMMER FIST STRIKE—This strike uses a "clubbing" effect on the intended target. Using a tightly-closed fist, strike downward (or sideways), multiple times at the body part that you are attacking.

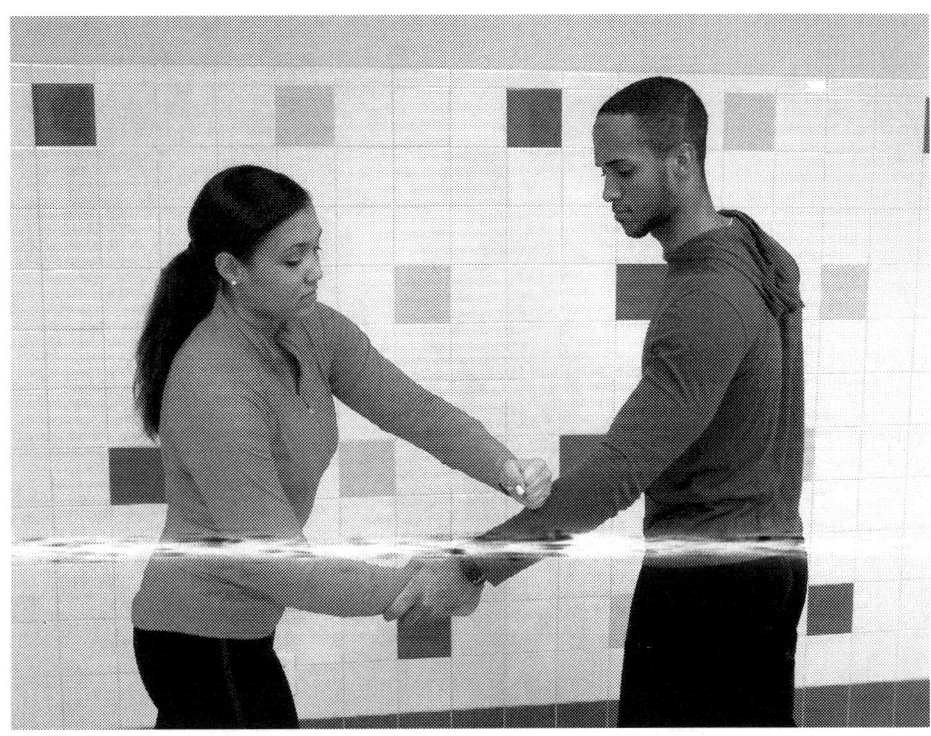

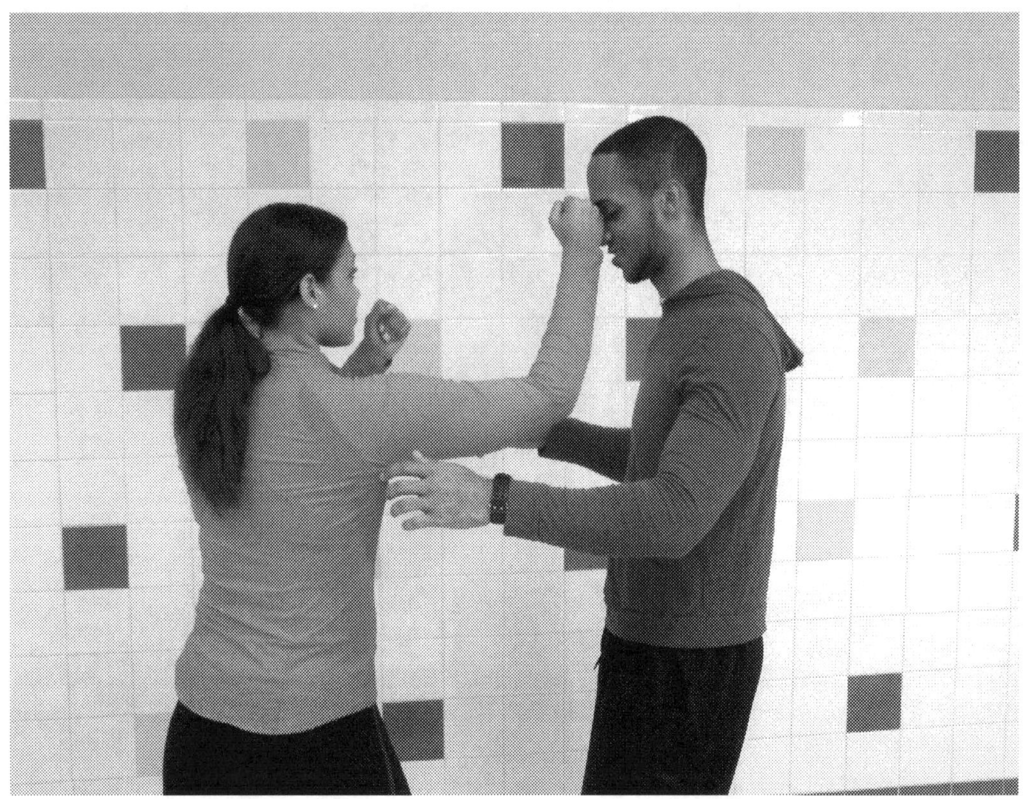

Matt using a Hammer Fist to the side of the head.

ELBOW STRIKES

FORWARD ELBOW STRIKE—From the fighting position, strike the aggressor standing in front of you with your elbow by swinging your elbow across the front of your body. Be sure to turn your palm toward the ground so that you strike with the point of your elbow. The target area is the face or body.

Morgan is using the lead elbow to strike while Matt is using the rear elbow.

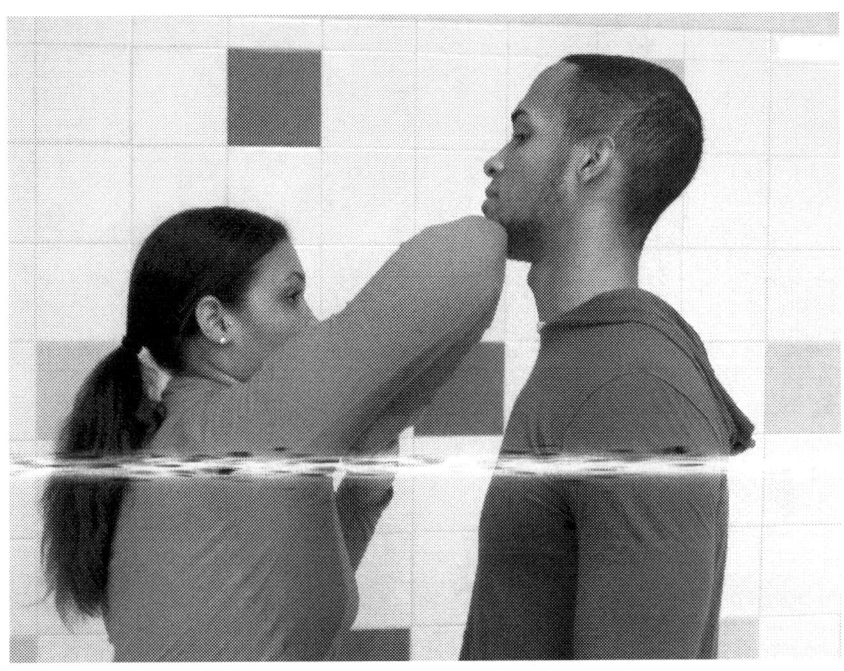

RISING ELBOW STRIKE—From the fighting position, strike the aggressor standing in front of you by swinging your elbow straight up in front of you. Be sure to turn your palm toward your ear as you strike upward. Your target area is the chest/sternum, and then the chin/face.

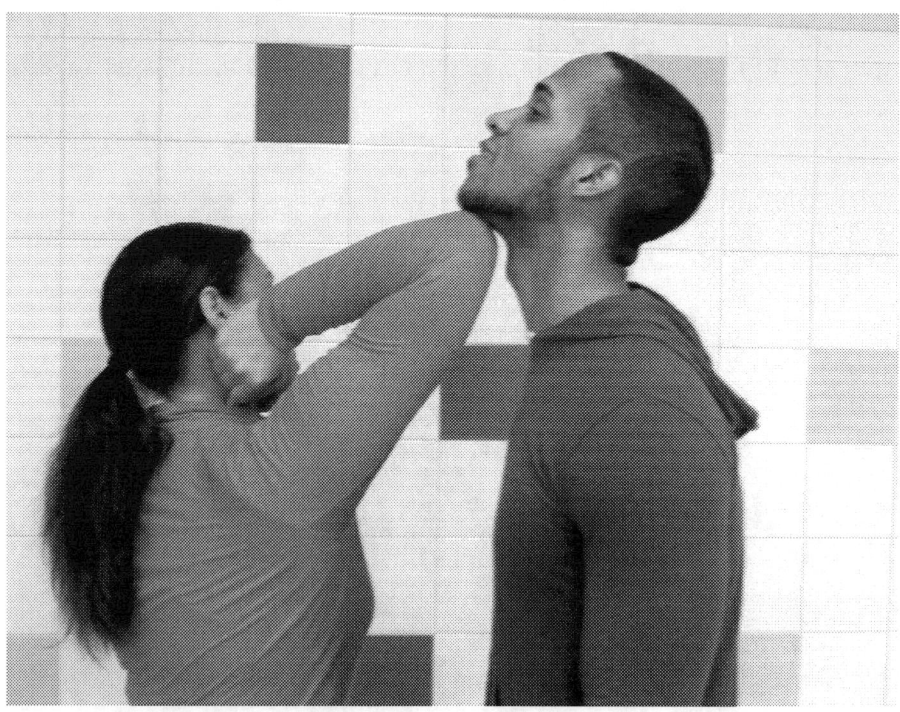

Rising Elbow Strike to the chin.

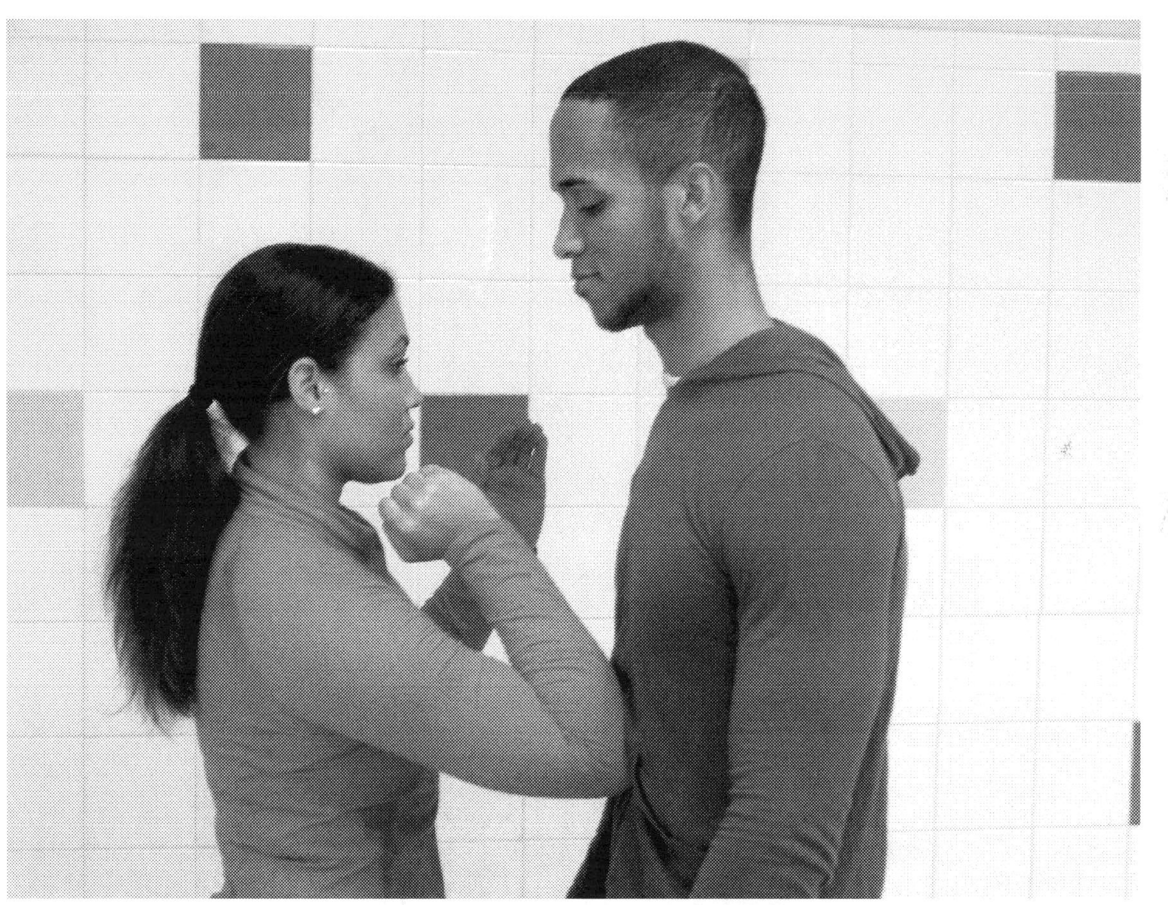

Rising Elbow strike to the chest.

SIDE ELBOW STRIKE—From the fighting position, strike the aggressor standing to either side with the elbow. Be sure to have your palm facing down so that you strike with the point of the elbow. Your target area is the head or torso. (This is a great technique from the seated position).

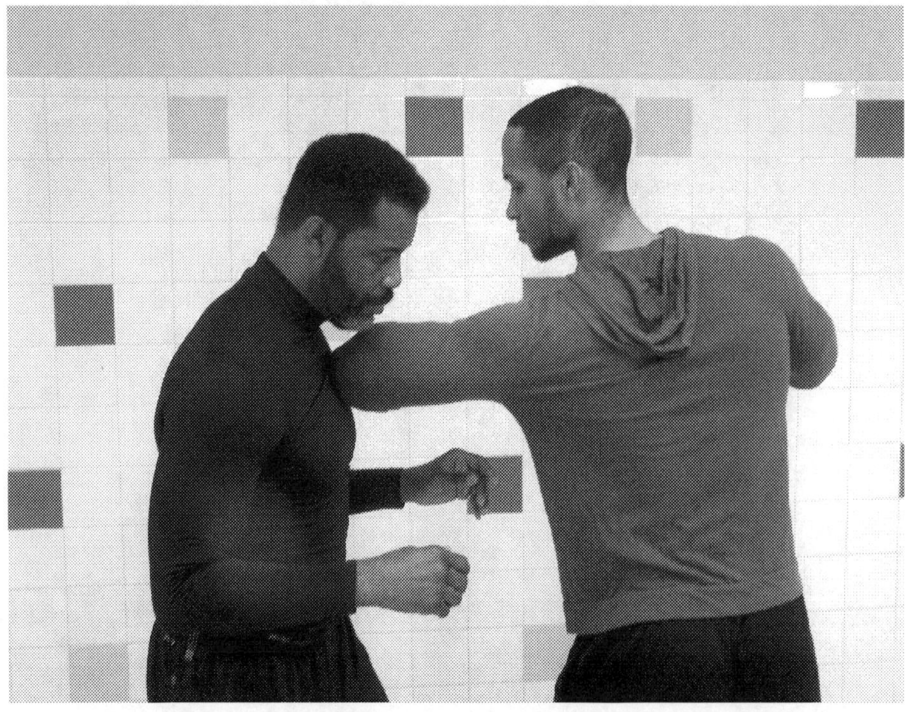

Matt delivers a Side Elbow Strike to the chest.

REAR ELBOW STRIKE (TO THE BODY) Turn slightly and look to the rear as you strike the aggressor standing directly behind with your elbows. Be sure to turn your palm upward so that the point of the elbow strikes the target area. Keep your elbow close to your body as you execute this technique. Your target area is the attacker's mid-section.

REAR ELBOW STRIKE (TO THE HEAD) This technique is designed to defend against an aggressor grabbing you from behind (with your arms free). When the aggressor grabs you, immediately drop your center, twist quickly at the waist, using your elbows to attack the aggressor's head. Be sure to have your palms are facing downward so that you strike with the point of your elbow.

DOWNWARD ELBOW STRIKE—This technique can be used in a variety of situations. With your palm facing you, raise your arm up as high as you can, then drive the point of the elbow down as hard as you can!

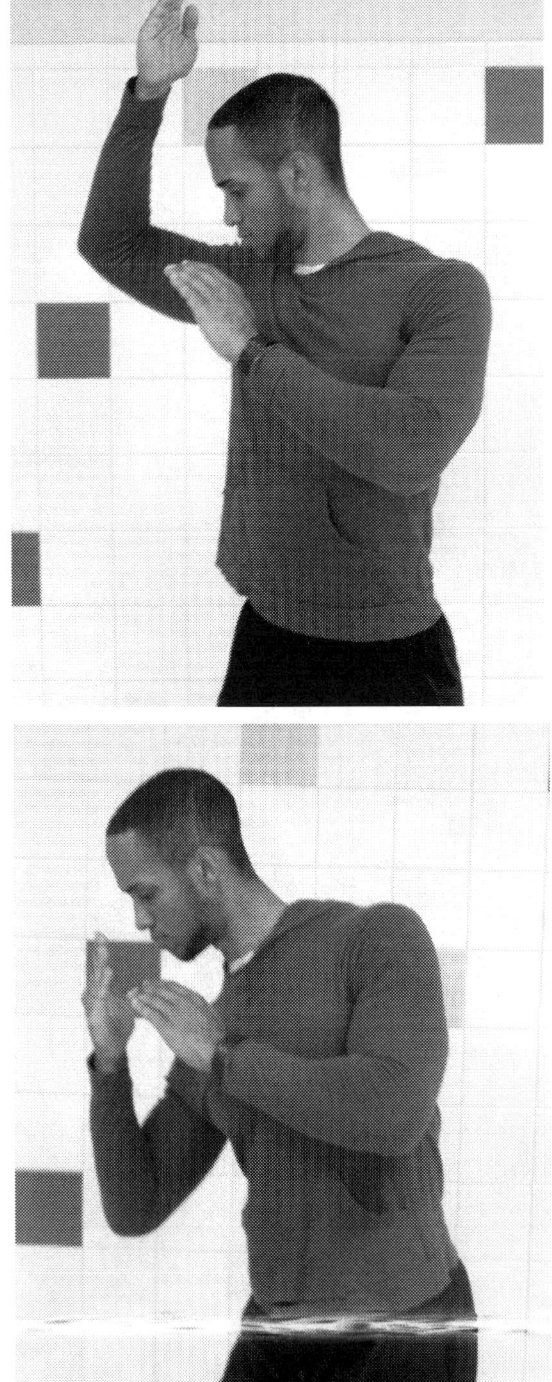

You can also use this technique if you are on you back on the ground.

This technique can be used to defend against an attempt by the aggressor to grab or tackle you. In the case of an attempt by the aggressor to tackle you, you should drop down into a wider stance and drive the point of your elbow into the aggressor's spine. Your goal is to force the aggressor to the ground.

GROIN CHOPS/STRIKES/GRAB—Groin Chops/Strikes/Grabs obviously are "close quarters" fighting tactics. They are typically used when the aggressor has grabbed you either from the front or rear and has your arms wrapped up.

Years ago when I first joined the police department the word got out that I was a Martial Artist. So several of the guys decided that it would be funny to grab me from behind in a bear hug and say, "What are you going to do now, Bruce Lee?" Well, a quick, but controlled chop to the groin immediately corrected that behavior. The word got out and people stopped testing me.

REAR GROIN CHOP/STRIKE/GRAB—Scenario #1: Picture yourself in a situation where the aggressor is standing directly behind you (such as a co-worker trying to get too familiar with you at an office party). Use the edge of your hand to chop backward and strike the aggressor's groin area. You can also use your closed fist to strike as well. Once you have struck the attacker in the groin, grab the testicles (if the attacker is a male), squeeze and hold until the aggression stops. *NOTE* If you have a friend or loved one that likes to test your skills, instead of striking them, you can grab and pinch the insides of their thighs and convince them to release you!

REAR GROIN CHOP/STRIKE/GRAB—Scenario #2: The aggressor has grabbed you in a bear hug from behind and your arms are pinned. The first thing that you are going to do is drop your center of gravity and take a wide stance for better balance. Lean slightly forward at the waist to keep from being easily lifted off of the ground. Immediately go to work! Chop/Strike/Grab the attacker's groin area as hard and fast as humanly possible! Continue the attack until the aggressor releases you and the aggression stops.

FRONT GROIN CHOP/STRIKE/GRAB—The scenarios and methods of defense are the same except the aggressor is in front of you instead of behind you.

NOTE When striking the aggressor with the Groin Chop, your goal is to lift him/her off of the ground with the force of the strike.

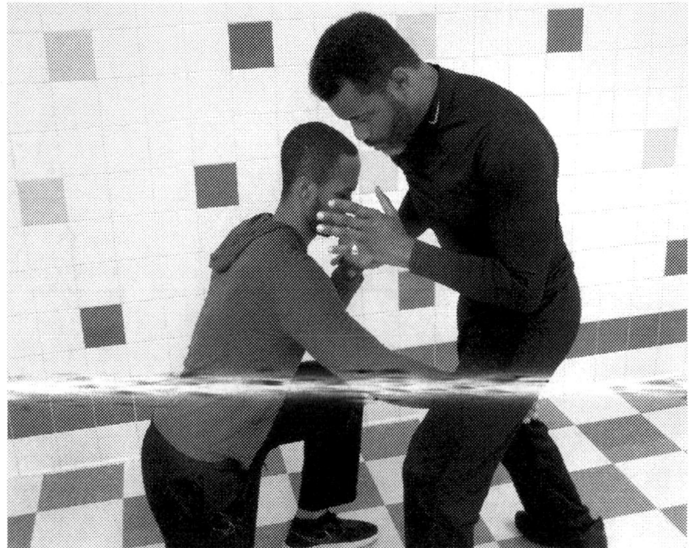

KNEE SPIKES—Knee Spikes are very effective in close-in fighting situations. Let's say that the aggressor has gotten too close to you and you are now in a grappling situation or a standing struggle. You can lock your wrists around the aggressor's neck, or grab some hair or clothing. Put one leg back as far as you can, then pull him/her down as you bring your knee upward. Be sure to keep your toe pointed down towards the ground. Deliver at least three strikes to the target. You can target the face, groin, mid-section, or thighs with this technique.

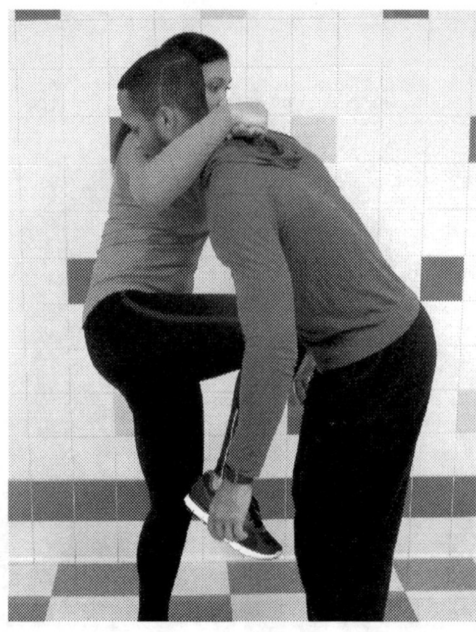

FRONT KICK—The Front Kick is perhaps the most simple and effective kick in a fighter's tool bag. I have used this kick numerous times with great success in the Dojo and on the streets in actual combat. From the fighting position, using your rear (strong side) leg, bring your knee up to the desired height and point it at the aggressor. Curl your toes back towards your body to keep your foot muscles tight. Snap your foot out and hard and quickly as possible at your target. Bring the foot back quickly and set it down to prepare to continue fighting if necessary. Make sure you get back a good fighting stance. When executing this kick, imagine yourself trapped in a burning room and you have to kick the door open in order to get out. That is how hard you should be kicking the aggressor.

Aim at the abdomen or lower. Draw the leg back quickly and get back in the fighting position.

Front Kick to the hip joint. This technique is very effective in stopping forward motion.

LEAD LEG FRONT KICK—This time you are using the front leg to quickly kick an aggressor that may have surprised you or is rushing towards you and you need to slow him/her down.

HEEL STOMP—This is an extremely close-in fighting technique best used when the aggressor has grabbed you or is too close for a good punch or kick. Bring either leg up several inches; turn your foot toes pointing outward, so that your heel becomes your primary weapon. Drive that heel downward as quickly and powerfully as possible onto the top of the aggressor's foot. Ladies, imagine that you are wearing five inch heels and driving through the aggressor's foot!

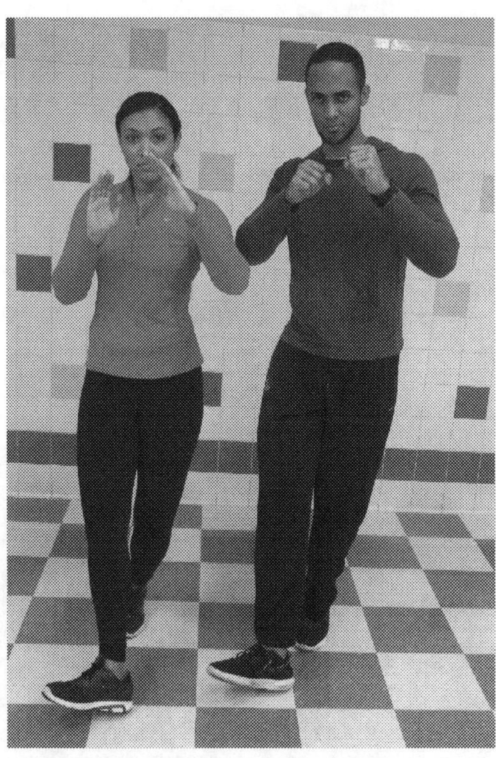

REAR HEEL STOMP—The aggressor is standing behind you or has grabbed you from behind. Using your heel, stomp down on the aggressor's foot as hard as possible.

HEEL KICK—The same as the Heel Stomp except that your kick outward instead of down.

HEEL KICK WITH SHIN SCRAPE—With this variation you put your shoe against the aggressor's shin and scrape forcefully down to the top of the foot.

UPWARD REAR HEEL KICK—This kick is borrowed from one of the Kung Fu styles. It looks funny but it can be very effective and difficult to detect. We practiced it in class on one of the dummies (none of the students seemed to want to be my demonstrator or have fellow students practice on them), and found it to be a very sneaky defense tool. The aggressor is standing behind you, you simply swing your heel back and up almost as if you were trying to hit your own behind, but you aim for the aggressor's groin. Some of the smaller students found that if they jump a little, they can deliver a pretty effective kick.

SIDE KICK—The Side Kick, when properly delivered is extremely effective and powerful. This version of the Side Kick is designed to stop attacks coming from the left or right side of your body. (You can use it in any direction by simply turning sideways to the threat). From the Fighting Position, raise your knee up to the front as if you were going to do a front kick. Be sure to pull your toes back. Quickly kick out to the side, using the bottom of your foot to strike the target. Bring the leg back into position set it down. Get back into your fighting position and prepared to continue the fight.

BACK KICK—This kick is designed to defend against an attacker standing behind you. From the fighting position, raise your knee up to the front just as if you were going to do a front or side kick. Pull your toes back. Look back as you lean slightly forward. Using the bottom of your foot, kick backward as quickly and forcefully as possible. Quickly bring the leg back and get back into fighting position to prepare for the next attack. (You may have to turn to face the threat after the kick). You can launch the kick without bringing the knee up once you get better accustomed to the technique.

*Remember to imagine that you are trying to kick a door open to escape a fire when launching this kick.

SECTION VII – SPECIALIZED STRIKES

"My actions are a result of your actions"
-BRUCE LEE

EYES/THROAT (DEADLY FORCE)

In certain situations, you may have to use what is considered "Deadly Force" to save your life or the life of another. Deadly Force is defined as: Force that likely to cause Death or Great Bodily Harm. Now I know that it is not a pleasant thought, but it could come down to it one day and therefore you must be prepared to not just survive, but win! You see, in my opinion, survivors hang on and barely make it through. Winners however, go all out, do whatever it takes, and give it their all with the intent to emerge victorious! I know that sometimes surviving is all you can do, but if you go in with the clear intent to win, you might just surprise yourself, and the aggressor!

Please refer to the Chart in Section XII for examples of Use of Force guidelines (as used by the Police).

EYE STRIKES

CAT'S CLAW OR CAT STRIKE—Using your fingertips, rake your fingers across downward across the aggressor's eyes.

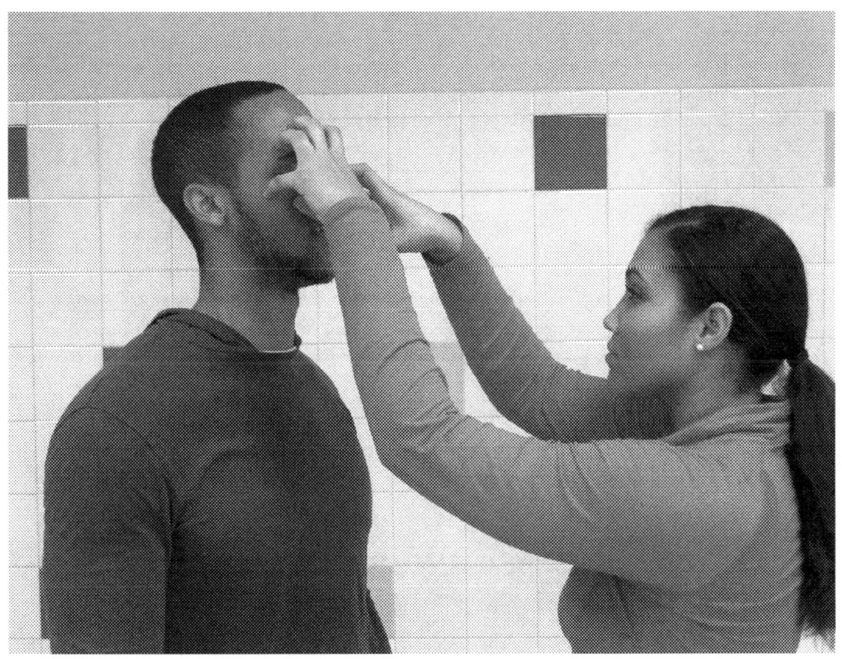

BIRD BEAK PECK—Put your thumb and fingers together so that they resemble a bird's beak. Use them to quickly and repeatedly jab the aggressor's eyes. (Much like a Woodpecker pecking at a tree).

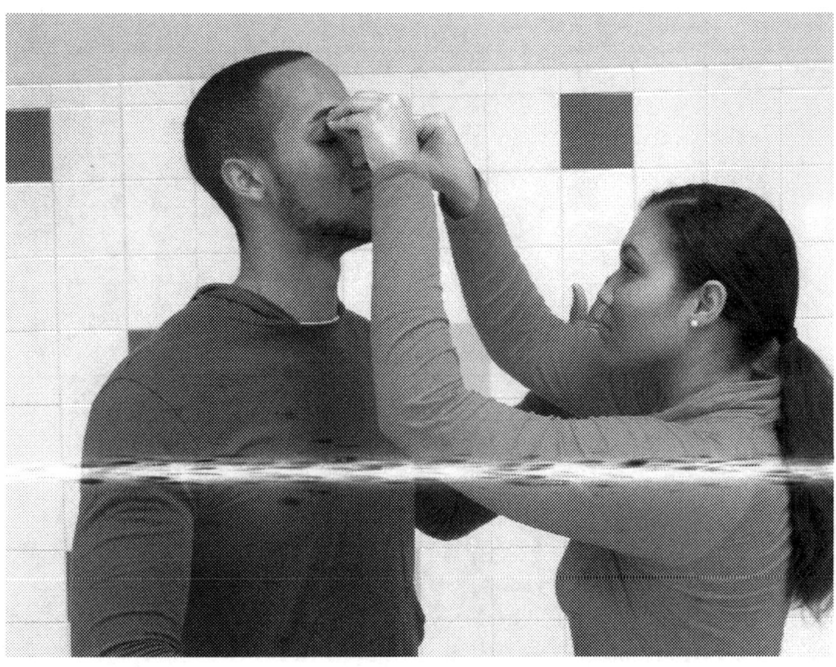

EYE GOUGE—Your life is in peril and you must act decisively! Place your thumbs, fingers, or whatever you can find on the aggressor's eyeballs and push forcefully.

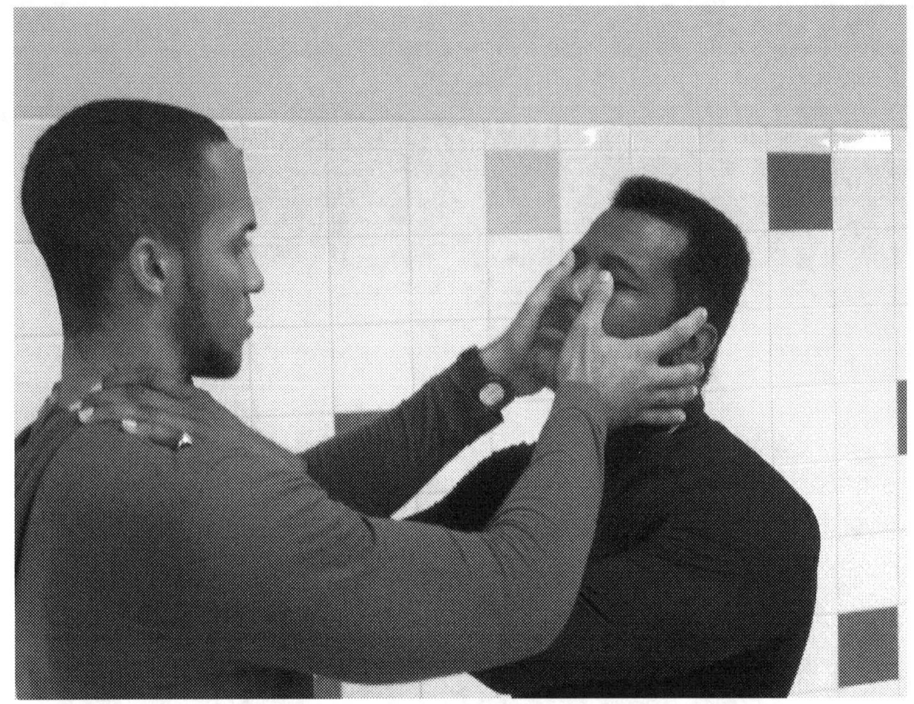

THROAT STRIKES

Any of the strikes or punches previously shown can be used to attack the throat area if Deadly Force is warranted. A simple grabbing and squeezing of the larynx can cause enough distress for the aggressor to cease an assault. An open hand slap across the throat can cause great distress as well (usually without causing permanent injury).

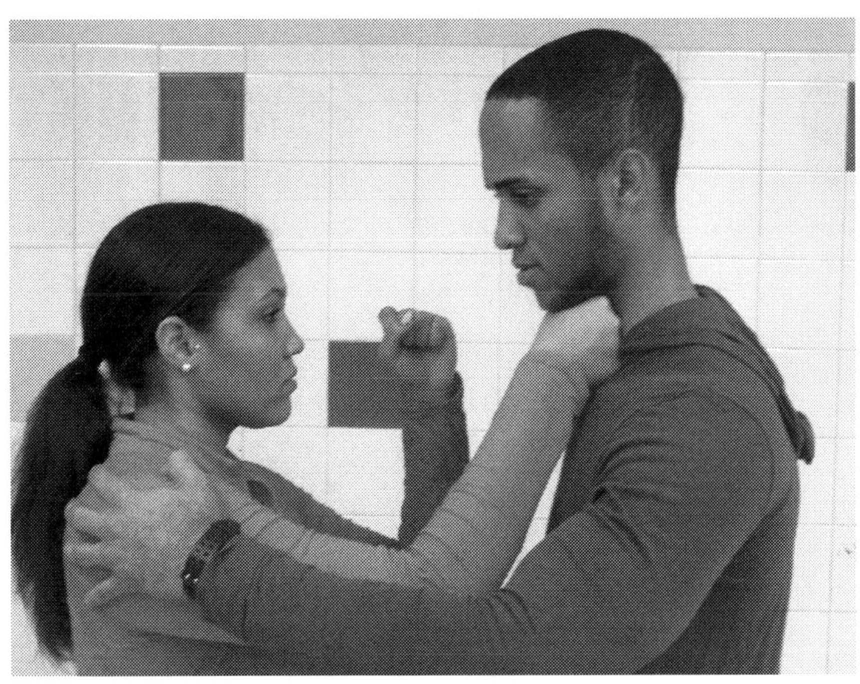

Remember, the aggressor may be drunk, high on illegal narcotics, or have an unusually high pain tolerance. One simple application of a technique may not work. Keep fighting and trying different techniques until the aggression stops!

Once again, these techniques are for ***SELF-DEFENSE*** or the ***LAWFUL DEFENSE*** of others only!! You must be able to articulate to the Police and a Judge why you used such force. I will be happy to testify on your behalf if you use these techniques to lawfully defend yourself against violent attack.

Anyone that uses these techniques ***UNLAWFULLY*** or in the ***COMMISSION OF A CRIME*** will and should face criminal prosecution! In this case, I ***MAY BE CALLED*** to assist in your prosecution!

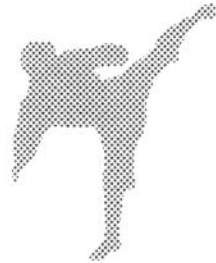

SECTION VIII – ESCAPES/FALLS /GROUND DEFENSE

"Fall down seven times, stand up eight"
—JAPANESE PROVERB

ESCAPES

OUTSIDE WRIST ROLL—This technique is used for a non-violent, but unwanted encounter such as a club scene or office setting. The aggressor has just grabbed your wrist. Calmly bring your arm up as if to check the time on your watch. Open your hand so that your palm is facing the aggressor. Push your hand towards to aggressor (palm still facing him/her). You will 'roll' your wrist slightly to the outside/away from your body as you push toward the aggressor. You can actually 'roll' your wrist and grab theirs as your break their hold.

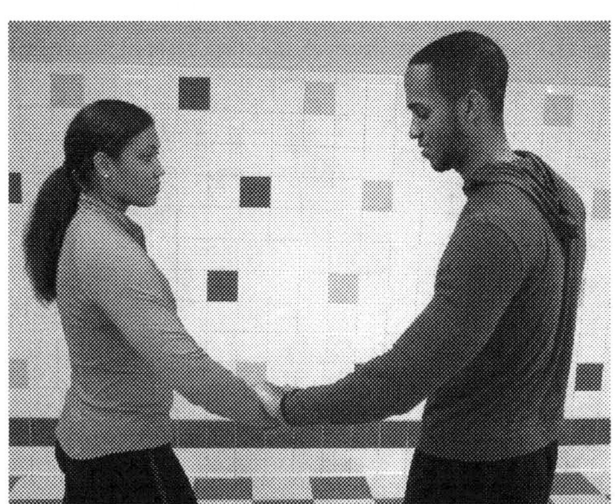

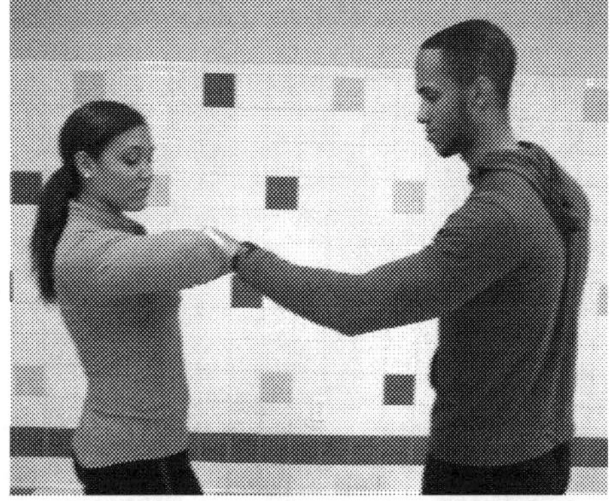

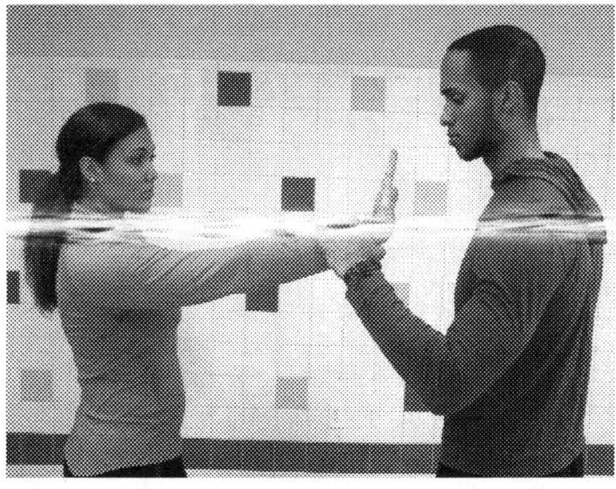

THUMB PEEL—This technique is often used by Dignitary Protection professional to pry open the hand of an over-zealous fan or groupie who has a grip on their client's hand. I actually had to use this on a woman who had a death-grip on Miss America's hand as we tried to make it through a large crowd. When the aggressor grabs you, firmly grab his/her thumb with your entire hand and peel it away from you.

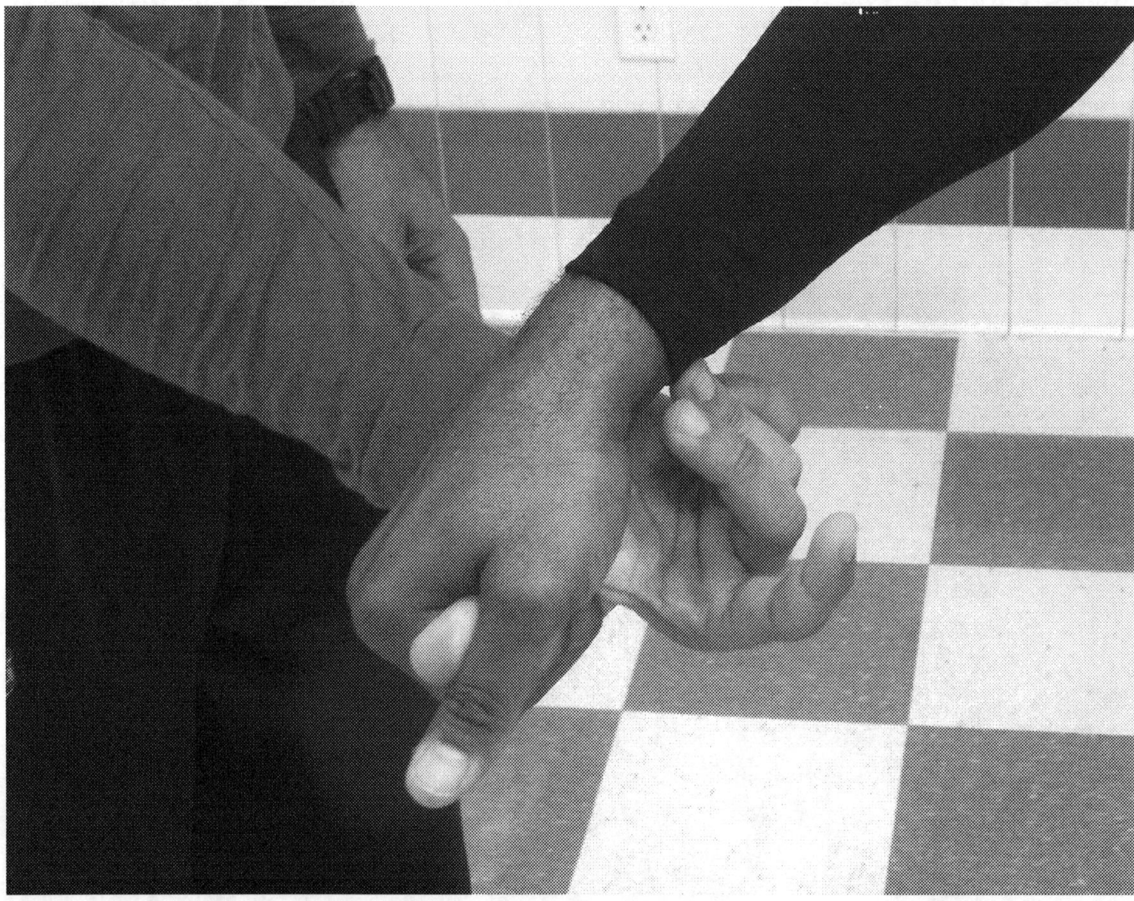

THUMB-SIDE SNATCH—Most grab/grips can be broken by quickly snatching away from the thumb side.

THUMB SIDE SNATCH AND PUSH—This technique is used for the more aggressive grabber. Quickly but smoothly bring your arm up as if to check the time on your watch (it doesn't matter if you're actually wearing one or not). Bring your other hand up and smack down on the aggressor's wrist as hard as possible. Be sure to keep your hands up and get some distance between you and the aggressor should he/she reacts violently.

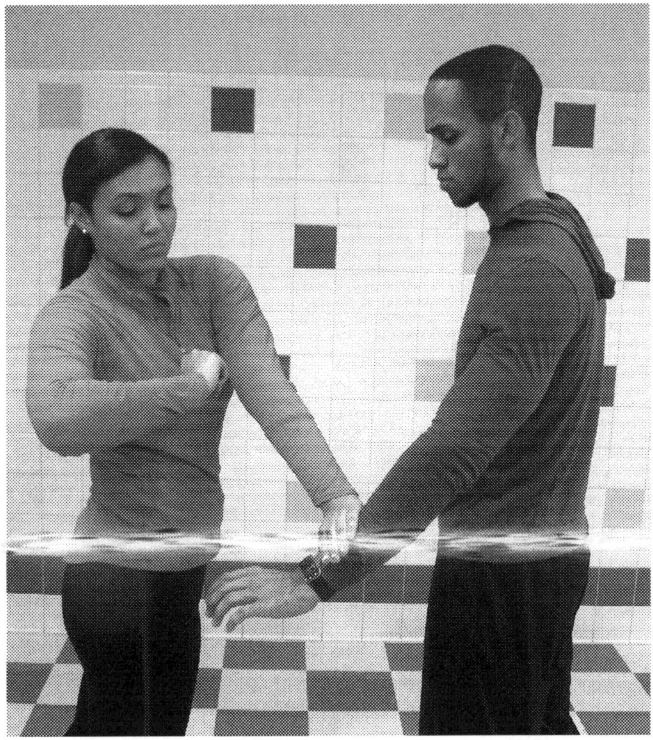

HAIR-PULL/GRAB DEFENSE—In this situation, you must immediately get into a good, solid stance and tighten your abdomen muscles so that you can't be easily dragged around. Having you hair pulled will be painful but not fatal, so focus and think! Now, put your hands up and assume the Emergency Block position to protect your head and face. Face towards the Aggressor and grab the wrist and/or forearm of the hand being used to grab your hair. Using your entire body, turn away from the Aggressor, twisting his/her arm until it is trapped between your arm and body. You now have several options: you can use a Back Kick to the Aggressor's body or legs. You can Rear Heel Stomp the Aggressor's feet, or you can use a Rear Elbow Strike to the Aggressor's face. You can also lock down the Aggressor's elbow joint and use pain compliance to force him/her to release you. If all else fails, you can bite their arm!!

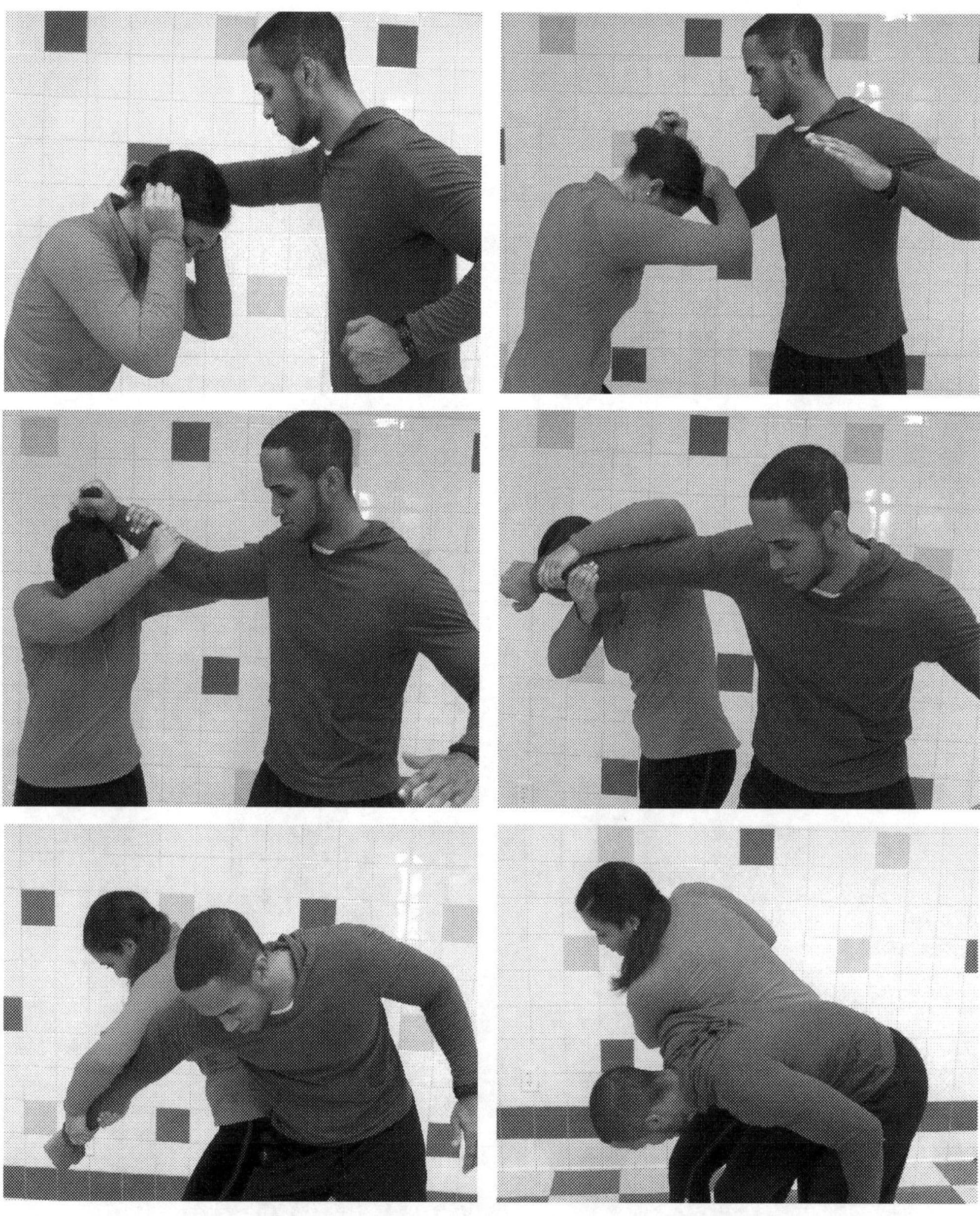

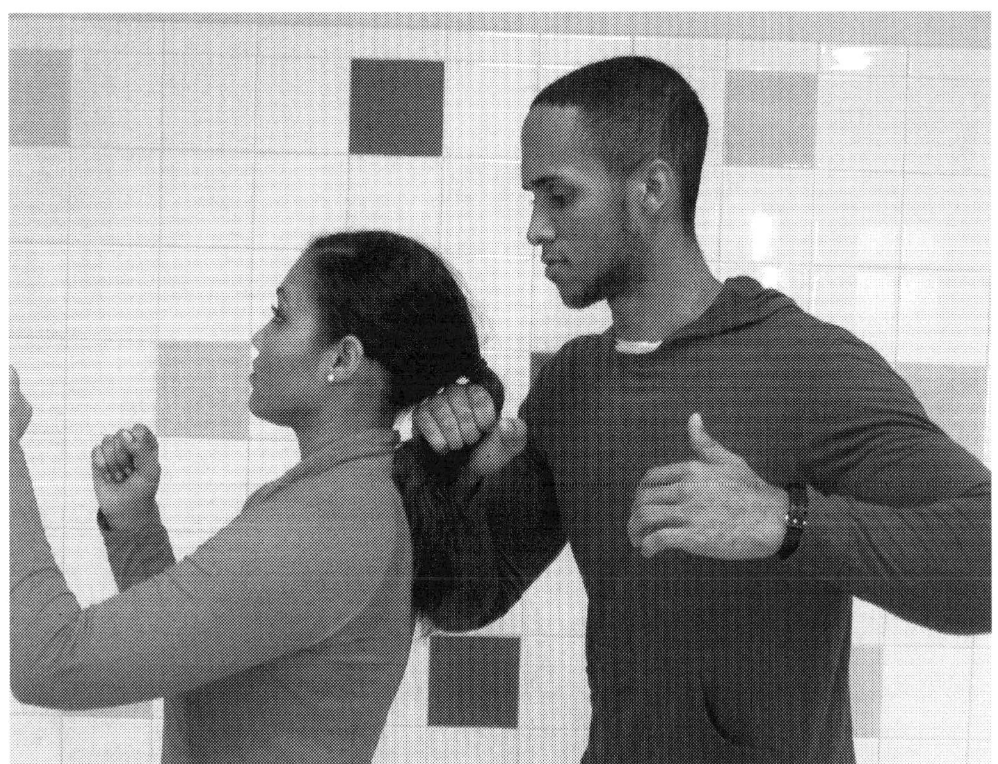

Matt has grabbed Morgan's hair from the rear.

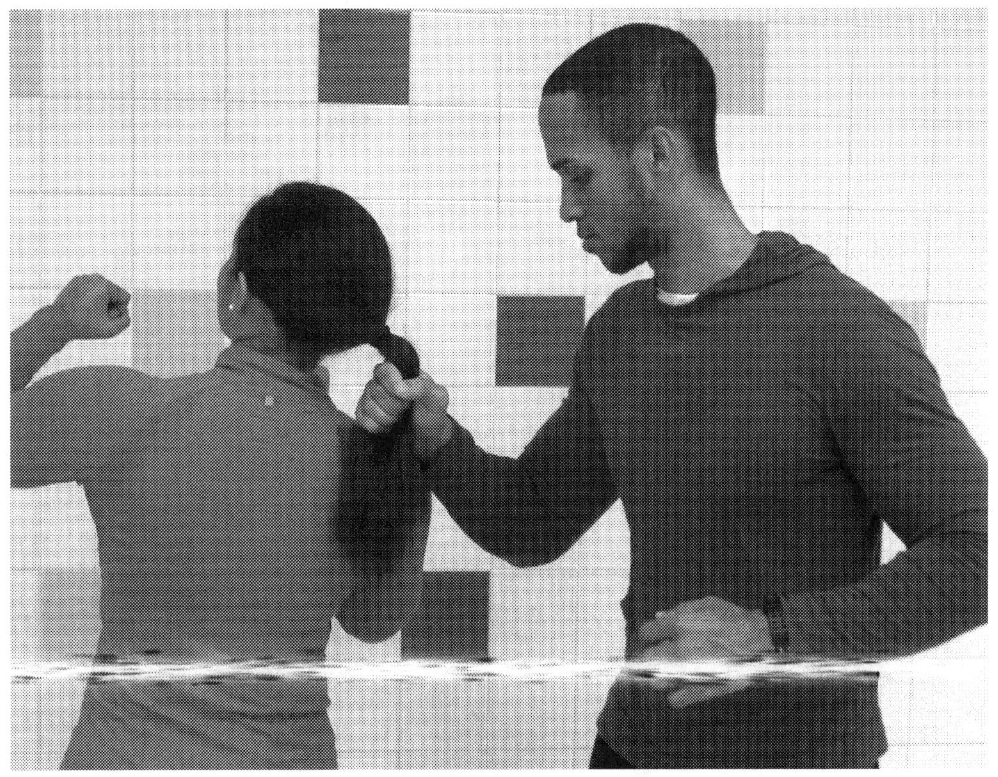

Step quickly to the outside of the attack.
Remember to widen your stance and maintain balance.

From here you have a variety of techniques that you can use to free yourself. You can attack the face, body, groin, or legs. Morgan has chosen to attack with a Cat Strike and a punch to the head.

FRONT CHOKE DEFENSE—The aggressor has grabbed you by the throat with his/her hands and is choking you! You have seconds before you pass out so you must act quickly! Get into a strong and wide stance and lower you center, tuck you chin down and raise your hands above your head. Turn quickly so that your side is towards the aggressor. This action should break or loosen his/her grip. You now have several options: You can strike the aggressor in the face multiple times with your elbow, or you can side kick him/her as hard as you can! Your goal is to stop the aggression and escape! DO NOT let them regain a chokehold!! You can also try raising your arms up and clasping your hands together and turning. This may give you some extra leverage. This technique also works if you are on your back. You may have to use painful distractor techniques such as biting, kicking, gouging, and scratching before breaking free. If the aggressor's grip is too powerful, try isolating one finger or thumb one each hand, and break them! Keep fighting until you are victorious and the aggression stops!! If you have any small weapons such as a knife, this is a good time to use them!! This technique also applies to a rear or side one or two-handed choke.

In the photos that follow, Morgan uses the basic technique. Matt uses the advanced technique where he reaches across his body and grabs one of the attacker's wrists. He holds on to the wrist while he breaks the Choke Hold so that he can put the attacker in an Arm Bar.

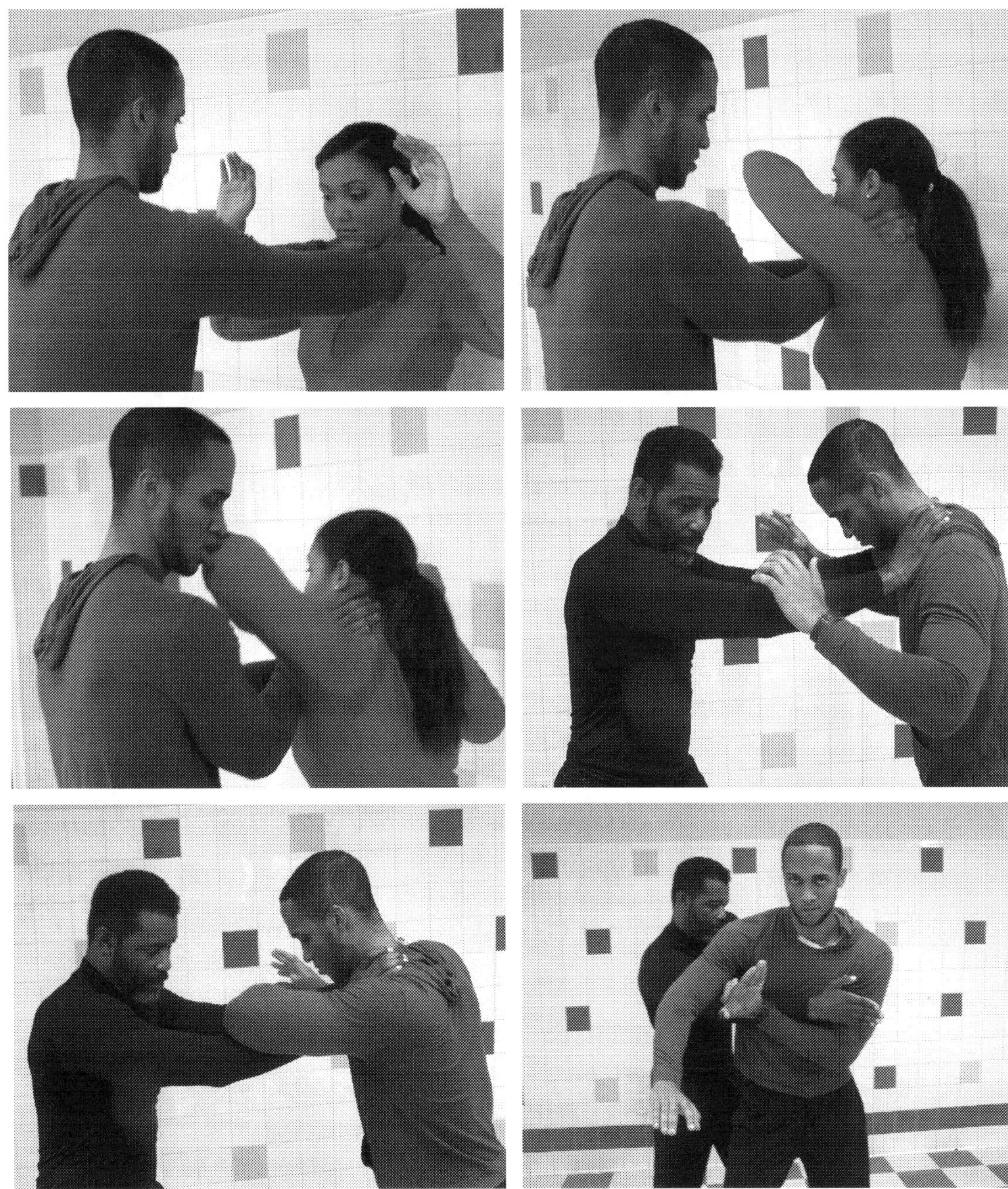

REAR CHOKE—Perhaps the most frightening of all of the chokes because the person is behind you with their arms around your neck. That fear is compounded when we see Professional Fighters using it to defeat each other in Gladiator matches on television. Remember, when the aggressor grabs us with both hands/arms, our hands are usually free to do all kinds of damage. You and I are not fighting in a ring with rules and a referee so we can do whatever it takes to win! No body part is off limits! We are at the Deadly Force Level because our lives are in danger!

WAR STORY: I was working the Downtown Bar Detail and was talking to three other officers when we heard a commotion behind us. We turned to see a smaller guy on the back of a larger guy. They large guy was face down on the sidewalk and the small guy was on top of him, holding him in a Rear Choke. My partner delivered a (perfect) Knee Spike to the aggressor's side and rolled them both over so that the small guy was now on the bottom. My partner hit the aggressor on the hip and did not cause enough pain compliance to cause the aggressor to release his grip on the victim's throat. We are now at the Deadly Force Level in our Force Continuum so I was completely justified in shooting the aggressor. I gave one final command for the aggressor to release the victim and again he refused. The victim is not moving now so I had to act fast. Instead of shooting the aggressor, I used a powerful kick to render him semi-conscious and stopped the aggression. The aggressor had attacked the victim from behind after losing a fight with him earlier. The victim made no viable attempt to save himself from a much smaller opponent. With a little training and practice, might have been able to escape his attacker. Although this is a frightening experience and many of my students were initially reluctant to try it, once they tried it and saw that it works, their fears quickly subsided.

The aggressor has grabbed you in a Rear Choke around the neck. The first thing you do is what we always do; get into a good, strong stance! Lean forward as much as you can and stand as wide as you can. Turn and tuck your chin into the crease of the aggressor's arm to protect your throat and prepare to bite him/her. Grab his/her arm on either side of their elbow and dig your fingernails in deep as you pull down. Position your body so that your butt is against his/her groin area. Using the arm that is around your neck, twist and pull that arm down towards the ground. This is an effective technique but it takes some practice. You will need a good mat to land on because the throw is quick and your partner will go down hard. (See the following photos).

If you don't think you can do the first technique, you have several options: you can use one hand to attack the body with elbow strikes or groin strikes; or you start biting, breaking fingers, or go for the throat and eyes. Remember, this is not a ring match, you are now fighting for your life! Go to work on the aggressor! If the aggressor tries to move you or pick you up, hook your leg around his/hers. Keep fighting until you are free and the aggression stops! Never give up! Never quit! Never stop!!

HEAD LOCK—This another situation that seems frightening but is much easier to get out of than you might imagine. Remember; when both of the aggressor's hands are occupied and yours are free, you can do a lot of damage. The first thing you need to do is get into a good wide stance and stabilize yourself. Then, turn you face towards their body and bite them or prepare to bite them. This will also protect you from being choked. Now place one hand on their thigh, and the other one on their lower back. This is called "checking". This will help calm you down and help keep them from throwing you to the ground. Quickly place the hand that is on their thigh behind their knee and with the other hand reach up and either grab their hair or shirt collar, or slip your hand underneath their chin and pull back as hard as you can while lifting their leg with your other hand. Pull and push them off to one side. You can also chose to start biting right away, use your free hand to attack the groin area, or deliver Knee Spikes to their leg. You can also push out of the head lock by pushing their elbow away from your head. (See photos). You should use a padded Training Mat for this technique because your partner will go down hard.

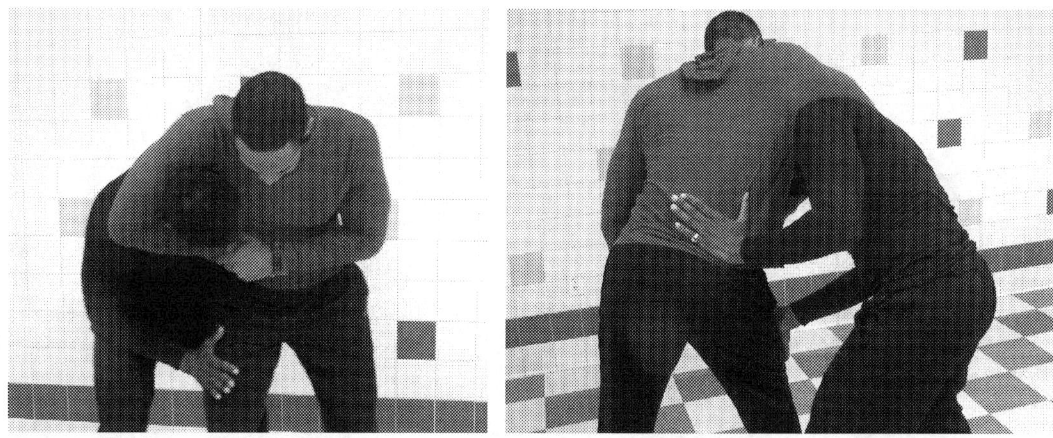

Turn your chin towards the aggressor. "Check" the aggressor by placing your hands as shown.

Cup the chin and the closest leg. Pull the chin back and lift the leg. Bite and scratch if you have to.

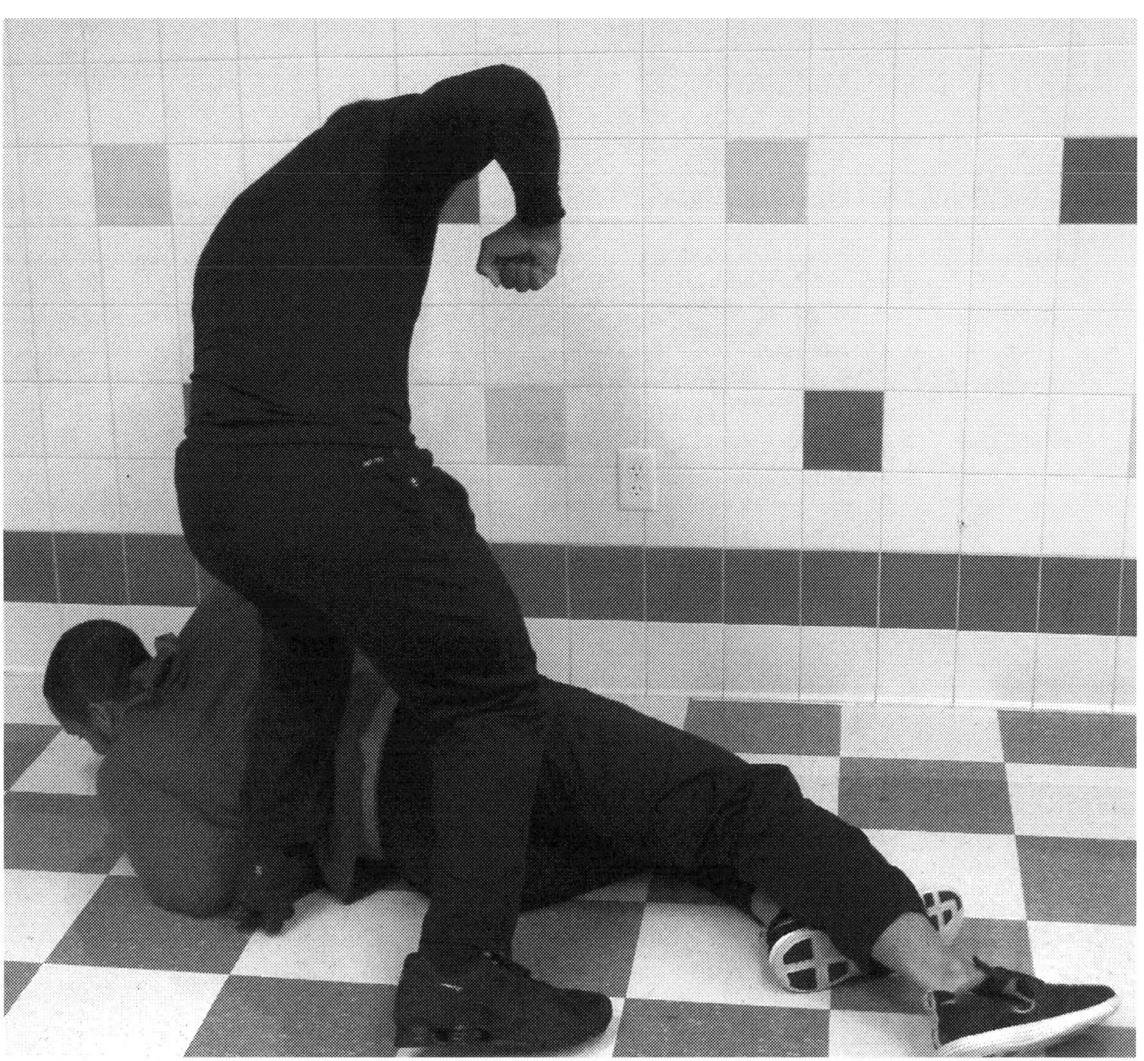

Finish the fight!

FRONT FALL—When falling forward, it important to try not hit your face on the floor/ pavement for obvious reasons. Should you fall forward or get pushed from behind, the position you land in should look just like the 'Plank' position in Yoga. The goal is not to let your face hit the ground and to land on your forearms, not your wrists and hands. This will minimize injury, allow you to recover quicker, and keep fighting. You should use a padded Training Mat, pillows, or your bed when practicing this fall.

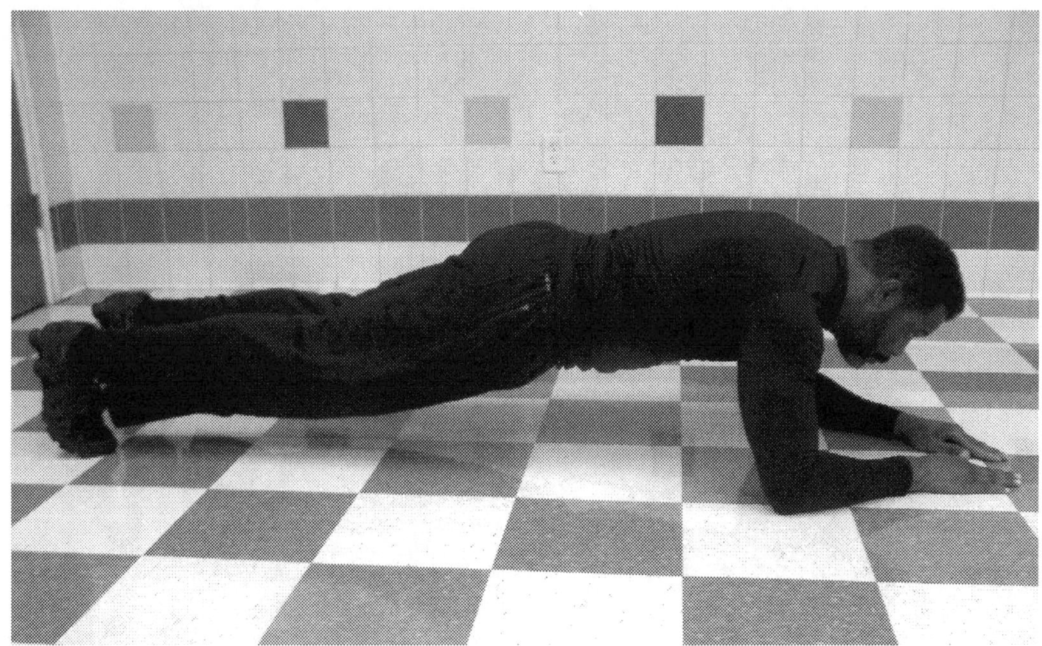

REAR FALL—When falling backward, it is critical that you do not hit your head and render yourself unconscious. Should you fall backward, immediately tuck your chin to your chest. This will keep you from hitting your head on the ground. Round your spine and tuck your knees as you go down so that you 'rock' when you land instead of slamming flat.

GROUND DEFENSE—Okay, so now you're on the ground because you fell or got knocked down. The goal here is to keep the aggressor off of you until you can get up safely. Roll to one side and prop yourself up on one arm. Keep your palm and forearm on the ground. Raise the other arm up along the side of your body for protection. Tuck the leg that is on the ground in so that the aggressor cannot step on it. Use your other leg to kick the aggressor as hard as you can if he/she gets too close. Get up as quickly as possible! Remember, this is not a wrestling or MMA match. If the aggressor somehow gets on top of you, kick, punch, bite, scratch, gouge, cut, stab, or shoot him/her until the aggression stops. Never give up! Never quit! Never stop! There is no such thing as a fair fight! Anyone that puts their hands on you against your will deserves everything they get!

Kick the knee or shin as hard as you can.

SECTION IX – COMBINATIONS DRILLS

"How you train is how you will perform."
-POLICE ACADEMY MOTTO

Now that you have the basics, let's put it all together with a few simple combination drills. These drills are designed to help you develop that critical muscle memory and information storage when a sudden attack occurs and you need to act quickly and decisively. You can practice alone or with a partner. Keep the pace nice and slow until you naturally develop more fluidity, speed, and skill.

Repetition is the mother of skill. Practice, then practice some more!

How to train: 1—For basic practice, do each technique ten times on the left side, then the right side.
2—For a more intense workout, do twenty five repetitions of each drill.

WARM UP—Do 25-50 jumping jacks or jog in place for several minutes before stretching. You can also do simple calisthenics to warm up. A short Yoga session will also warm you up for practice.

Assume a good fighting stance and let's begin.

High Block, Palm Strike, Front Kick

Middle Block, Vertical Punch, Front Kick

Deflector Block, Double Palm Strike, Lead Leg Front Kick

Low Block, Vertical Punch, Front Kick to the Shin, Double Palm Strike

High Block, Double Vertical Punch, Side Kick (turn sideways to the aggressor and kick)

Middle Block, Double-Tap Palm Strike, Front Kick to the Shin, Knee Spike

Deflector Block, Double Palm Strike, Front Kick

Low Block, Vertical Punch, Side Kick

Emergency Block, Heel Stomp, Double Palm Strike

Rear Elbow to the Body, Rear Groin Chop, Back Kick or Rear Heel Kick or Rear Heel Stomp

Rear Elbow to the Head, Rear Elbow to the Body, Rear Groin Chop, Back Kick or Rear Heel Kick or Heel Stomp

High Block, Eye Attack, Heel Stomp, Rising Elbow Strike, Double Palm Strike

Left Side Elbow Strike (head or body), Left Side Kick

Right Side Elbow Strike (head or body), Right Side Kick

Middle Block, Elbow to the head, Heel Stomp, Knee Spike

High Block, Eye Attack, Elbow to the Head, Knee Spike

Middle Block, Rising Elbow Strike, Elbow to the Body, Front Groin Chop

Middle Block, Side Elbow (left or right), Side Kick

High Block, Eye Attack, Front Groin Chop or Kick, Knee Spike

High Block, Eye or Throat Attack, Heel Stomp, Elbow to the Head

Low Block, Double-Tap Vertical Punch, Front Kick, Side Kick

Always remember to return to a good solid stance when executing techniques.

You can use a chair or wall to keep your balance when you practice your kicks.

THE FRONT KICK

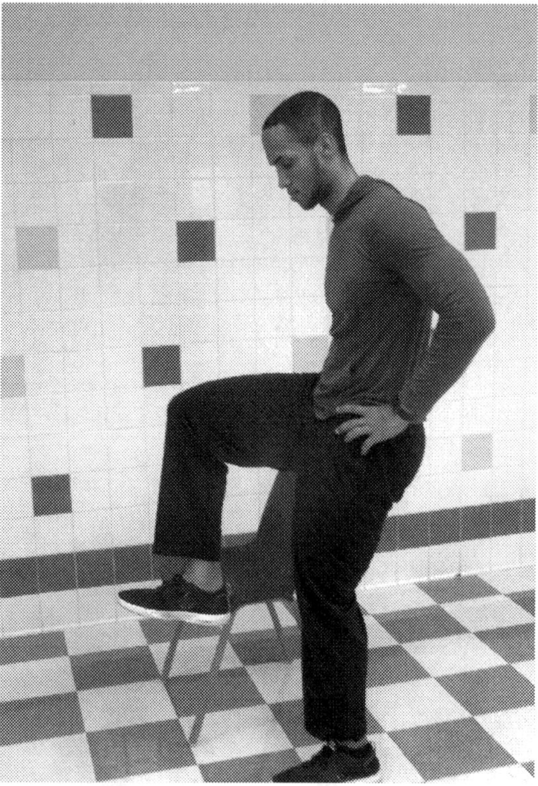

THE SIDE KICK

TO PRACTICE PROPER FORM, RAISE THE KNEE TO THE FRONT.

HOLD ON AS YOU KICK STRAIGHT OUT TO THE SIDE. RETURN TO THE ORIGINAL POSITION.

THE BACK KICK

TO PRACTICE PROPER FORM, RAISE THE KNEE STRAIGHT UP TO FRONT.

KICK STRAIGHT BACK, USING THE CHAIR FOR SUPPORT. RETURN TO THE ORIGINAL POSITION. YOU CAN ALSO "MULE KICK" STRAIGHT BACK (WITHOUT RAISING THE KNEE FORWARD). THE MULE KICK IS QUICKER BUT LESS POWERFUL.

SECTION X – REPORT WRITING

"Are you smarter than a fifth grader?"
-TELEVISION GAME SHOW

So many times I have taken the statement of a victim and no matter what their level of education, the statement is generally lacking in what the Police and Courts need to properly prosecute a criminal. Police Officers are usually trained to write their reports on a Third Grade level so that they are easily understood by everyone that has to read them. In other words, Keep It Simple! The problem with most adults is that unless you write for a living, you will have to be coached on how to write a proper, court-worthy police statement. Not to worry, we will fix that right now.

The document on the next page is a Statement form used by the Orlando Police Department. All agencies use the same basic format for witness/victim statements.

There are two critical things that the police need to make an arrest and present the case to the State Attorney's Office.

1. The fact that a crime was actually committed. The elements of the crime must be in the victim's statement.
2. The willingness to prosecute. The victim must demonstrate and/or state in writing that he/she is willing to prosecute. The exception is in Domestic Violence cases where the officer does not ask if the victim wants to prosecute or write a statement. Since the victim is usually emotionally attached and often controlled by the aggressor, the officer makes an arrest based on the evidence available to him/her at the scene.

This is just a basic sampling of how a report should be written.

On Monday, September 1, 0000, at 1130 pm, I pulled into the driveway of my home and parked my car. I turned the car off and was about to get out when my cell phone beeped to let me know that I had an incoming text. I got my phone and answered the text. When I looked up there was man standing at my door. He opened the door, reached in and pulled me out. He said, "Don't scream or I will kill you!" He was holding a silver gun in his right hand. He reached into the car and grabbed my purse off of the seat. He took my phone and told me to get on the ground. I got down on the ground and he told me to stay there or he would shoot me. He got into my car and drove away. I looked up and saw another car leaving with him. I ran into the house and called the police. [Now at this point you will add in the suspect's description, race, sex, height, weight, etc . . .] You will also have to add in all the information about what was stolen from you. You will have to say if you can recognize the suspect if you see him/her again. Then, finally, you will have to say if you are willing to prosecute and testify in court.

Of course, this is just a short example of what your statement might look like. The more details you give; the better case you build against the criminal once he/she is caught. I have attached a blank copy of a police statement for familiarization purposes.

POLICE DEPARTMENT

Case #:

Statement

Please fill out in full detail

Date of Statement:	Month:	Day:	Year:	Time:
Offense:				
Date of Offense:	Month:	Day:	Year:	Time:

Suspect (last, first, middle):

Location of Offense:					District:
Person Code:	Name (last, first, middle):	Age:	DOB:	Race:	Sex:
	Address Residence:	Zip:	Phone:		
	Address Business:	Zip:	Phone:		
	Email Address:				
Type of ID shown:	ID# if applicable:				

I, ______________________________________, do hereby voluntarily make the following statement without threat, coercion, offer of benefit, or favor by any persons whomsoever.

Sworn to and subscribed before me, this ___ day of __________, ________

____

Notary Public ☐ Law Enforcement Officer ☐ Name Key

Personally Known ☐ Produced Identification ☐ Type_____________

I swear/affirm the above and/or attached statements are correct and true.

Signature: ________________________________

My signature below means that I refuse to prosecute the person(s) named above for the alleged crime(s) that occurred to me or to the property un

Signature________________________Date______________

(Departmental policy prohibits use of this section in domestic violence cases.)

Victim Rights Booklet provided? Yes ☐ No ☐

I will testify in court and prosecute criminally. Initials:

Miranda Warning Read? Yes ☐ No ☐

Page _____ of _____

1113.9 6/7/11 White: Staw: Records

POLICE DEPARTMENT

Case #:

Statement

(CONTINUED)

Sworn to and subscribed before me, this ___ day of __________, ______

____ ______

Notary Public ☐ Law Enforcement Officer ☐ Name Key

I swear/affirm the above and/or attached statements are correct and true.

Signature: ________________________________

Page _____ of _____

1113.9 6/7/11 White: Staw: Records

SECTION XI – BULLYING

"Learn to do right. seek justice. free the oppressed, and correct the oppressor . . ."
-ISIAIH 1:17

Bullying it seems, has been around since there were more than two humans walking the Earth. It is pervasive in our society and shows no signs of subsiding anytime soon. However, with the advent of video cameras, cell phones, and the Internet, it has come to light in a most disturbing way. It seems that it is human nature to prey on those perceived to be weaker or different than what is normally accepted by society. What is frightening and sad about that scenario is that we have done little to aggressively and properly protect those who cannot protect themselves. In our modern society, failure to address this critical issue often ends in a heartbreaking suicide, or catastrophic violence in the form of an Active Shooter.

Legislators are now passing laws that are designed to address those issues, but like Domestic Violence, laws and paper can only protect you so much. I often hear others say; "Just walk away." That sounds all well and good when you are not in the situation. But when you are faced with eminent violence from an obvious or perceived threat, sometimes the last thing you want to do or should do is turn your back on it. Studies of several wars have shown that soldiers became more aggressive and attacked more when the enemy turned and ran. In my own situation as a victim of bullying, it did not stop until I stood my ground. I am not saying that you have to do what I did, but in the absence of proper adult or lawful intervention or protective measures, one must be prepared to defend oneself from Interpersonal Human Aggression. If you are the victim of bullying, take steps to protect yourself. Here's how:

1. Document every word and deed the aggressor says and does from the beginning. Start a journal right away!
2. Write a statement. 'On Tuesday, April 1st, 1234, at 1130, I was standing at my locker getting a book out and talking to Billy. Big Mike came up behind me and pushed my face into the locker. I fell down. Big Mike put his hand in my pocket and took my lunch money. My lip was bleeding.' Now by law, this is a Strong-Arm Robbery and should be reported to the police. Take that statement that you just wrote and make copies. Give one to your teacher and one to your parents. Do this every time you are harassed. Call the police if no other adult will help you. Don't give up! Fight for your rights!

3. Practice Escape and Evasion. Plan your travel routes. Know where the bully hangs out and where he/she might try to attack you. For instance, if you ride the same bus as a group of bullies that want to hurt you, refuse to ride the bus. That will force the adults to take action.
4. Learn to defend yourself both physically and intellectually. Learn Self-Defense and use the legal system to your advantage. Your main weapon is your mind. Use it.

Listed below is the Florida State Statute on Bullying. The laws in your state may be different.

1006.147 BULLYING AND HARASSMENT prohibited.—

(1) This section may be cited as the "Jeffrey Johnston Stand Up for All Students Act."
(2) Bullying or harassment of any student or employee of a public K-12 educational institution is prohibited:
 (a) During any education program or activity conducted by a public K-12 educational institution;
 (b) During any school-related or school-sponsored program or activity or on a school bus of a public K-12 educational institution; or
 (c) Through the use of data or computer software that is accessed through a computer, computer system, or computer network of a public K-12 educational institution.

(3) For purposes of this section:
 (a) "Bullying" means systematically and chronically inflicting physical hurt or psychological distress on one or more students and may involve:
  1. Teasing;
  2. Social exclusion;
  3. Threat;
  4. Intimidation;
  5. Stalking;
  6. Physical violence;
  7. Theft;
  8. Sexual, religious, or racial harassment;
  9. Public humiliation; or
  10. Destruction of property.

 (b) "Harassment" means any threatening, insulting, or dehumanizing gesture, use of data or computer software, or written, verbal, or physical conduct directed against a student or school employee that:
  1. Places a student or school employee in reasonable fear of harm to his or her person or damage to his or her property;
  2. Has the effect of substantially interfering with a student's educational performance, opportunities, or benefits; or
  3. Has the effect of substantially disrupting the orderly operation of a school.

(c) Definitions in s. 815.03 and the definition in s. 784.048(1)(d) relating to stalking are applicable to this section.

(d) The definitions of "bullying" and "harassment" include:

1. Retaliation against a student or school employee by another student or school employee for asserting or alleging an act of bullying or harassment. Reporting an act of bullying or harassment that is not made in good faith is considered retaliation.
2. Perpetuation of conduct listed in paragraph (a) or paragraph (b) by an individual or group with intent to demean, dehumanize, embarrass, or cause physical harm to a student or school employee by:
   a. Incitement or coercion;
   b. Accessing or knowingly causing or providing access to data or computer software through a computer, computer system, or computer network within the scope of the district school system; or
   c. Acting in a manner that has an effect substantially similar to the effect of bullying or harassment.

SOURCE: FLORIDA STATE STATUES

SECTION XII – ANATOMY AND FORCE CONTINUUM CHART

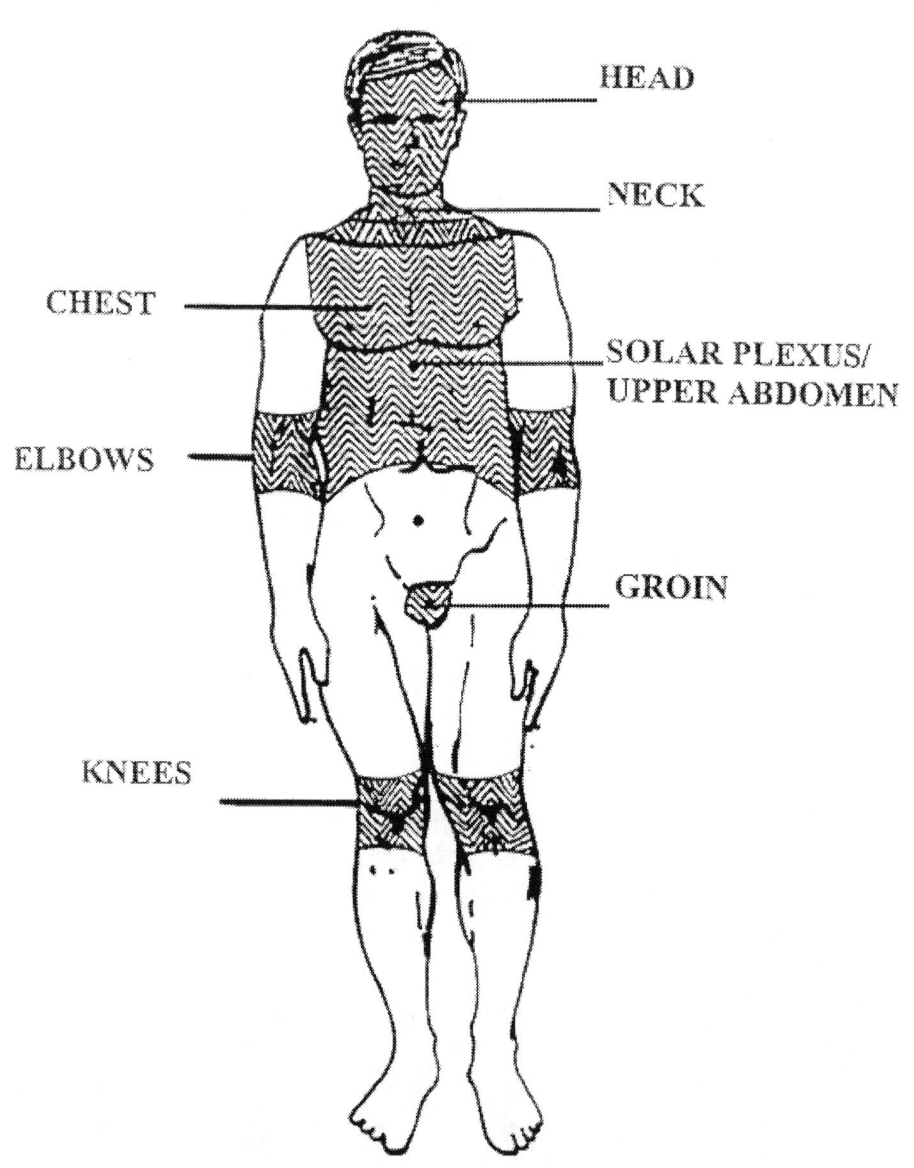

ATTACHMENT "A"
RESISTANCE AND RESPONSE CONTINUUM

SUSPECT'S RESISTANCE	EMPLOYEE'S RESPONSE
LEVEL I—INDICATORS OF RESISTANCE Non-verbal cues indicating subject's demeanor and attitude coupled with an apparent readiness to resist.	**EMPLOYEE'S PRESENCE** The employee's attitude and demeanor and their lawful right to be where they are.
LEVEL II—VERBAL RESISTANCE The subject's verbal responses indicating non-compliance and unwillingness to cooperate	**VERBAL DIRECTIONS** The employee's verbal communications that specifically direct the actions of the subject and offer the opportunity for compliance.
LEVEL III—PASSIVE RESISTANCE The subject fails to obey verbal direction preventing the member from taking lawful action.	**SOFT CONTROL** The employee applies techniques that have a minimal potential for injury to the subject, if the subject resists the technique.
LEVEL IV—ACTIVE RESISTANCE The subject's actions are intended to facilitate an escape or prevent an arrest. The action is not likely to cause injury.	**HARD CONTROL** The member applies techniques that could result in greater injury to the subject, if the subject resists their application by the member.
LEVEL V—AGGRESSIVE RESISTANCE The subject has battered, or is about to batter a person/member and the subject's action is likely to cause injury.	**INTENSIFIED TECHNIQUES** Those techniques necessary to overcome the actions of the subject, short of deadly force. If the subject resists or continues to resist these techniques there is a strong probability of injury being incurred by the subject.
LEVEL VI—DEADLY FORCE RESISTANCE The subject's actions are likely to cause death or great bodily harm to the member or another person	**DEADLY FORCE** Member's actions may result in death or great bodily harm to the subject.

OTHER FACTORS THAT HAVE TO BE CONSIDERED:

AGE

SEX

SIZE

SKILL LEVEL (REMEMEBR THE NAVY SEAL?)

MULTIPLE SUBJECTS OR EMPLOYEES

SPECIAL CIRCUMSTANCES:

MENTAL INCAPACITY/CLOSEPROXIMITY TO FIREARM OR WEAPONS/DISABILITY/ IMMINENT DANGER/ALCOHOL OR DRUG INFLUENCE/

This section is just for familiarization purposes and to show you what Police Officers' guidelines are when they are required to use force of an aggressor. You are by no means bound by these rules but it is a good baseline for how you to be familiar with.

SECTION XIII – DOMESTIC VIOLENCE

"Will you take the pain I give you again and again?"
-STRANGELOVE, BY DEPECHE MODE

Incidents of Domestic Violence seem to be occurring at a horrifying rate nationwide. It is a seemingly unstoppable epidemic of murder and brutal attacks with no end in sight! In the city where I work, nine women and one man were gunned down in less than a month. The killers, all estranged husbands or ex-boyfriends killed several people at once or within a very short time span. Domestic Violence cases here are up over 100 percent. Women are being beaten, choked, and murdered in record numbers. Even as I write this paragraph, I am watching CNN cover a story about a man that shot and killed his wife over their divorce settlement. Maybe it is time for a new type of response. This book is not going to get into the Psychology behind being a victim of Domestic Violence and how difficult it is for them to break away from being isolated, verbally berated, shoved, punched, choked, and kicked by someone who claims to love them. Instead, we will offer you some suggestions on what to do when you do finally decide to break free of the batterer/ abuser.

You should always report Domestic Violence to the Police. You should always tell someone. You should always get an Injunction for protection against repeat violence or a restraining order. Then, you should plan your escape, defense, and prepare for battle.

In some extreme cases, the Domestic Batterer will respond violently when he/she is served an Injunction and/or Divorce papers. In these cases the victim's life could be in danger. If you are a Domestic Violence victim, you know the person that you are involved with. You know their mindset and what they are capable of. When you plan to leave them, plan for what you know; then plan for what you would never expect them to do. If you have an ex-whatever that has a propensity for extreme violence, you must take action to defend yourself. Too many times I have had to rescue someone being held hostage by a violent mate. Too many times I have seen women kidnapped and/or murdered by a mate that had a well-documented history of high-level violence. Typically, the battered mate/ victim takes woefully inadequate steps to protect themselves. First of all, a Restraining Order, while necessary, is only a piece of paper. If you hold it up in front of you while someone is shooting at you or trying to stab you; it will not save you from injury. If you have a mate that is capable of or has threatened deadly violence, here are several things that you must do to survive/win:

1. Move to an undisclosed location. Disappear off of his/her radar. Do not go to places where he/she knows or expects you to go. Leave town if you have to and are able to.
2. Change or leave your current employer. Many women are killed at work or kidnapped from where they work. I can tell you story after story about women killed in the workplace because the batterer knows that they will go to work. Too many times women are concerned with keeping a job when their very lives are in danger, and end up dead.
3. Plan ahead. Plan all of your legal strategies secretly. Plan your escape secretly. Plan to protect yourself with deadly force if necessary. Plan, Plan, Plan!
4. Purchase some type of defensive weapon that will save your life. Practice using that weapon. Visualize yourself in a violent confrontation with the batterer and winning. If you are planning on leaving a violent and potentially murderous mate, prepare for war!
5. Once you are out, don't go back! Take everything you need before you leave! That includes the pets. If you have to go back, take the Police with you. Do not take your sister, cousin, girlfriend, or mother! Only the Police have the tools and training to protect you from a violent abuser!
6. Dump your phone! Get a new phone immediately! Cellular phones are easily tracked, particularly if you share an account with the abuser. Stay off of your computer and social network sites. The abuser could be tracking your emails without your knowledge. Check your car for tracking devices. An Abuser can easily place a tracking device on your vehicle and keep tabs on you. If you took anything from the house, check it. Don't take any chances!

Listed below are the Florida State Statutes on Domestic Violence. The laws where you live may be different.

DOMESTIC VIOLENCE; definitions.—As used in ss. 741.28-741.31:

(1) "Department" means the Florida Department of Law Enforcement.
(2) "Domestic violence" means any assault, aggravated assault, battery, aggravated battery, sexual assault, sexual battery, stalking, aggravated stalking, kidnapping, false imprisonment, or any criminal offense resulting in physical injury or death of one family or household member by another family or household member.
(3) "Family or household member" means spouses, former spouses, persons related by blood or marriage, persons who are presently residing together as if a family or who have resided together in the past as if a family, and persons who are parents of a child in common regardless of whether they have been married. With the exception of persons who have a child in common, the family or household members must be currently residing or have in the past resided together in the same single dwelling unit.

"DATING VIOLENCE" means violence between individuals who have or have had a continuing and significant relationship of a romantic or intimate nature. The existence of such a relationship shall be determined based on the consideration of the following factors:

1. A dating relationship must have existed within the past 6 months;
2. The nature of the relationship must have been characterized by the expectation of affection or sexual involvement between the parties; and
3. The frequency and type of interaction between the persons involved in the relationship must have included that the persons have been involved over time and on a continuous basis during the course of the relationship.

SECTION XIV – CRIMES

"There are some men who just want to watch the world burn"
-ALFRED—BATMAN BEGINS

There are many instances where the criminal commits a crime just for the sake of committing a crime. There may be no underlying reason for it. It may be that their depraved mind is simply fulfilling a desire to wreak havoc and cause harm to you and/or society in general. We will talk about the criminal mind in the next section. This section is just to familiarize you with the different types of crimes, penalties, and their legal definitions. The laws and penalties where you live could be different.

Listed here are the most common crimes

ASSAULT—(1) An Assault is an intentional, unlawful threat by word or act to do violence to the person of another, coupled with the apparent ability to do so, and doing some act which creates a well-founded fear in such other person that violence is imminent. (2) Whoever commits an Assault shall be guilty of a misdemeanor of the second degree, punishable as provided in s. 775.082 or s. 775.083

AGGRAVATED ASSAULT—(1) An Aggravated Assault is an Assault: (a) With a deadly weapon without intent to kill; or (b) With intent to commit a felony. (2) Whoever commits an Aggravated Assault shall be guilty of a felony of the third degree, punishable as provided in s. 775.082, or s. 775.084

BATTERY—The offense of Battery occurs when a person: 1.Actually and intentionally touches or strikes a person against the will of the other; or 2.Intentionally causes bodily harm to another person. A person who commits a Battery commits a misdemeanor of the first degree, punishable as provided in s. 775.082, or s. 775.083.

FELONY BATTERY; DOMESTIC BATTERY BY STRANGULATION—1. A person commits Felony Battery if he or she: (a) Actually and intentionally touches or strikes the other person against the will of the other; and (b) Causes great bodily harm, permanent disability, or permanent disfigurement.
2. (a) A person commits Domestic Battery by Strangulation if the person knowingly and intentionally, against the will of another, impedes the normal breathing or circulation of the blood of a family or household member or a person with whom he or she is in a dating relationship, so as to create a risk or cause great bodily harm by applying pressure

to the throat or neck of the other person or by blocking the nose or mouth of the other person. (b) A person who commits Felony Battery or Domestic Battery by Strangulation commits a felony of the third degree, punishable as provided in s. 775.082, or s. 775.083, or s. 775.084.

AGGRAVATED BATTERY—

(a) A person commits Aggravated Battery who, in committing Battery:
   1. Intentionally or knowingly causes great bodily harm, permanent disability, or permanent disfigurement; or
   2. Uses a deadly weapon.

(b) A person commits Aggravated Battery if the person who was the victim of the Battery was pregnant at the time of the offense and the offender knew or should have known that the victim was pregnant.

Whoever commits Aggravated Battery shall be guilty of a felony of the second degree, punishable as provided in s. 775.082, or s. 775.083, or s. 775.084

SOURCE: FLORIDA STATE STAUTES

BURGLARY—1. Entering a dwelling, a structure, or a conveyance with the intent to commit an offense therein, unless the premises are at the time open to the public or the defendant is licensed or invited to enter; or

2. Notwithstanding a licensed or invited entry, remaining in a dwelling, structure, or conveyance:
   a. Surreptitiously, with the intent to commit an offense therein;
   b. After permission to remain therein has been withdrawn, with the intent to commit an offense therein; or
   c. To commit or attempt to commit a forcible felony, as defined in s. 776.08.

(2) Burglary is a felony of the first degree, punishable by imprisonment for a term of years not exceeding life imprisonment or as provided in s. 775.082, s. 775.083

FALSE IMPRISONMENT; false imprisonment of child under age 13, aggravating circumstances.—

(1) (a) The term "false imprisonment" means forcibly, by threat, or secretly confining, abducting, imprisoning, or restraining another person without lawful authority and against her or his will.
   (b) Confinement of a child under the age of 13 is against her or his will within the meaning of this section if such confinement is without the consent of her or his parent or legal guardian.

(2) A person who commits the offense of false imprisonment is guilty of a felony of the third degree, punishable as provided in s. 775.082, s. 775.083, or s. 775.084.

KIDNAPPING; kidnapping of child under age 13, aggravating circumstances.—

(1)(a) The term "kidnapping" means forcibly, secretly, or by threat confining, abducting, or imprisoning another person against her or his will and without lawful authority, with intent to:

1. Hold for ransom or reward or as a shield or hostage.
2. Commit or facilitate commission of any felony.
3. Inflict bodily harm upon or to terrorize the victim or another person.
4. Interfere with the performance of any governmental or political function.

(b) Confinement of a child under the age of 13 is against her or his will within the meaning of this subsection if such confinement is without the consent of her or his parent or legal guardian.

(2) A person who kidnaps a person is guilty of a felony of the first degree, punishable by imprisonment for a term of years not exceeding life or as provided in s. 775.082, s. 775.083, or s. 775.084.

ROBBERY.—

(1) "Robbery" means the taking of money or other property which may be the subject of larceny from the person or custody of another, with intent to either permanently or temporarily deprive the person or the owner of the money or other property, when in the course of the taking there is the use of force, violence, assault, or putting in fear.

(2) (a) If in the course of committing the robbery the offender carried a firearm or other deadly weapon, then the robbery is a felony of the first degree, punishable by imprisonment for a term of years not exceeding life imprisonment or as provided in s. 775.082, s. 775.083, or s. 775.084.

(b) If in the course of committing the robbery the offender carried a weapon, then the robbery is a felony of the first degree, punishable as provided in s. 775.082, s. 775.083, or s. 775.084.

(c) If in the course of committing the robbery the offender carried no firearm, deadly weapon, or other weapon, then the robbery is a felony of the second degree, punishable as provided in s. 775.082, s. 775.083, or s. 775.084.

SOURCE: FLORIDA STATE STUTUES

ROBBERY BY SUDDEN SNATCHING.—

(1) "Robbery by sudden snatching" means the taking of money or other property from the victim's person, with intent to permanently or temporarily deprive the victim or the owner of the money or other property, when, in the course of the taking, the victim was or became aware of the taking. In order to satisfy this definition, it is not necessary to show that:

(a) The offender used any amount of force beyond that effort necessary to obtain possession of the money or other property; or

(b) There was any resistance offered by the victim to the offender or that there was injury to the victim's person.

(2) (a) If, in the course of committing a robbery by sudden snatching, the offender carried a firearm or other deadly weapon, the robbery by sudden snatching is a felony of the second degree, punishable as provided in s. 775.082, s. 775.083, or s. 775.084.
(b) If, in the course of committing a robbery by sudden snatching, the offender carried no firearm or other deadly weapon, the robbery by sudden snatching is a felony of the third degree, punishable as provided in s. 775.082, s. 775.083, or s. 775.084.

HOME-INVASION ROBBERY.—

(1) "Home-invasion robbery" means any robbery that occurs when the offender enters a dwelling with the intent to commit a robbery, and does commit a robbery of the occupants therein.
(2) (a) If in the course of committing the home-invasion robbery the person carries a firearm or other deadly weapon, the person commits a felony of the first degree, punishable by imprisonment for a term of years not exceeding life imprisonment as provided in s. 775.082, s. 775.083, or s. 775.084.
(b) If in the course of committing the home-invasion robbery the person carries a weapon, the person commits a felony of the first degree, punishable as provided in s. 775.082, s. 775.083, or s. 775.084.
(c) If in the course of committing the home-invasion robbery the person carries no firearm, deadly weapon, or other weapon, the person commits a felony of the first degree, punishable as provided in s. 775.082, s. 775.083, or s. 775.084.

SEXUAL BATTERY.—

(1) As used in this chapter:
(a) "Consent" means intelligent, knowing, and voluntary consent and does not include coerced submission. "Consent" shall not be deemed or construed to mean the failure by the alleged victim to offer physical resistance to the offender.
(b) "Mentally defective" means a mental disease or defect which renders a person temporarily or permanently incapable of appraising the nature of his or her conduct.
(c) "Mentally incapacitated" means temporarily incapable of appraising or controlling a person's own conduct due to the influence of a narcotic, anesthetic, or intoxicating substance administered without his or her consent or due to any other act committed upon that person without his or her consent.
(d) "Offender" means a person accused of a sexual offense in violation of a provision of this chapter.
(e) "Physically helpless" means unconscious, asleep, or for any other reason physically unable to communicate unwillingness to an act.
(f) "Retaliation" includes, but is not limited to, threats of future physical punishment, kidnapping, false imprisonment or forcible confinement, or extortion.
(g) "Serious personal injury" means great bodily harm or pain, permanent disability, or permanent disfigurement.
(h) "Sexual battery" means oral, anal, or vaginal penetration by, or union with, the sexual organ of another or the anal or vaginal penetration of another by any

other object; however, sexual battery does not include an act done for a bona fide medical purpose.

(i) "Victim" means a person who has been the object of a sexual offense.

(j) "Physically incapacitated" means bodily impaired or handicapped and substantially limited in ability to resist or flee.

(2) (a) A person 18 years of age or older who commits sexual battery upon, or in an attempt to commit sexual battery injures the sexual organs of, a person less than 12 years of age commits a capital felony, punishable as provided in ss. 775.082 and 921.141.

(b) A person less than 18 years of age who commits sexual battery upon, or in an attempt to commit sexual battery injures the sexual organs of, a person less than 12 years of age commits a life felony, punishable as provided in s. 775.082, s. 775.083, s. 775.084, or s. 794.0115.

(3) A person who commits sexual battery upon a person 12 years of age or older, without that person's consent, and in the process thereof uses or threatens to use a deadly weapon or uses actual physical force likely to cause serious personal injury commits a life felony, punishable as provided in s. 775.082, s. 775.083, s. 775.084, or s. 794.0115.

(4) A person who commits sexual battery upon a person 12 years of age or older without that person's consent, under any of the following circumstances, commits a felony of the first degree, punishable as provided in s. 775.082, s. 775.083, s. 775.084, or s. 794.0115:

(a) When the victim is physically helpless to resist.

(b) When the offender coerces the victim to submit by threatening to use force or violence likely to cause serious personal injury on the victim, and the victim reasonably believes that the offender has the present ability to execute the threat.

(c) When the offender coerces the victim to submit by threatening to retaliate against the victim, or any other person, and the victim reasonably believes that the offender has the ability to execute the threat in the future.

(d) When the offender, without the prior knowledge or consent of the victim, administers or has knowledge of someone else administering to the victim any narcotic, anesthetic, or other intoxicating substance which mentally or physically incapacitates the victim.

(e) When the victim is mentally defective and the offender has reason to believe this or has actual knowledge of this fact.

(f) When the victim is physically incapacitated.

STALKING—definitions; penalties.—

(1) As used in this section, the term:

(a) "Harass" means to engage in a course of conduct directed at a specific person which causes substantial emotional distress to that person and serves no legitimate purpose.

(b) "Course of conduct" means a pattern of conduct composed of a series of acts over a period of time, however short, which evidences a continuity of purpose. The term does not include constitutionally protected activity such as picketing or other organized protests.

(c) "Credible threat" means a verbal or nonverbal threat, or a combination of the two, including threats delivered by electronic communication or implied by a pattern of conduct, which places the person who is the target of the threat in reasonable fear for his or her safety or the safety of his or her family members or individuals closely associated with the person, and which is made with the apparent ability to carry out the threat to cause such harm. It is not necessary to prove that the person making the threat had the intent to actually carry out the threat. The present incarceration of the person making the threat is not a bar to prosecution under this section.

(d) "Cyberstalk" means to engage in a course of conduct to communicate, or to cause to be communicated, words, images, or language by or through the use of electronic mail or electronic communication, directed at a specific person, causing substantial emotional distress to that person and serving no legitimate purpose.

(2) A person who willfully, maliciously, and repeatedly follows, harasses, or cyberstalks another person commits the offense of stalking, a misdemeanor of the first degree, punishable as provided in s. 775.082 or s. 775.083.

(3) A person who willfully, maliciously, and repeatedly follows, harasses, or cyberstalks another person and makes a credible threat to that person commits the offense of aggravated stalking, a felony of the third degree, punishable as provided in s. 775.082, s. 775.083, or s. 775.084.

SOURCE: FLORIDA STATE STATUTES

SECTION XV – CRIMINALS

"Son, there are some men who don't care if the sun comes up the next morning"
-JUNIUS BRADLEY SR

That is what my father told me just before I left for the Army. I didn't really understand what he was talking about. The concept of someone being that cold-blooded didn't really register in my young mind. Then, while talking Criminal Justice classes at the college near my base in California, I decided to write a paper on Charles Manson for my class assignment. It was then that I realized what my father meant. As my Military career progressed, I got involved in Counterterrorism and understood even more. But it wasn't until I became a Police Officer that I began to deal with the inner workings of the criminal mind and criminal behavior on a daily basis. As I engaged different types of criminals, from Terrorists to Transients, I see a very similar behavioral pattern. They are all absolutely convinced that they have a right to do whatever crime that they are doing, and they absolutely convinced of their own superiority.

As I said earlier, I didn't try to rationalize why terrorists did what they did. I did study their causes and their ideology to get an understanding of their methodology. Their political, religious, or ideological beliefs while, important for planning purposes; had no bearing on the level of my planned tactical response. In other words; whatever it is that drove them was irrelevant. The only thing that mattered that they were committing a crime and that my job was to stop them.

The same goes for street criminals. I am not really interested in why they are committing the crime at the time of the incident. I am not interested that he/she was abused as a child, or he/she wasn't hugged by their mother, or their father dropped them on their heads as little children. I am not concerned with anything other than that person is committing a crime and that I must stop them. Of course there are many variables that come into play in the Law Enforcement world that you the citizen don't have to worry about. So I say to you; don't ask why they are committing a crime. Don't think about it. Act! Defend yourself in the moment! I have added some excerpts from articles written in Psychology Today that may help you better understand the criminal mind.

Remember what I said earlier about how the criminal doesn't care about you or your life status? Read on . . .

A Criminal's Sentimentality Is Not Empathy

Again, appearance belies reality
Published on October 19, 2012 by Stanton E. Samenow, Ph.D. in Inside the Criminal Mind

- "I can change from tears to ice and back again," said a man who had committed many types of crimes, including rape. This was in fact an accurate observation. This individual had a soft spot for animals. He would nurse an injured dog to health. He would become teary eyed during movies that were sad. And he was deeply moved by church services that he attended regularly. Nonetheless, when it came to his intended victims, there was not a shred of empathy.
- I recall interviewing a murderer who refused to step on an insect because he "didn't want to kill anything living." Yet, after gunning down a total stranger (who he later learned was a husband and father of two children) during a robbery, he did not experience a moment of remorse.
- When I began evaluating and counseling offenders, I was struck by the intensity and sincerity of their sentimentality — so much so that I believed that the sentimentality could be capitalized upon as a motivator for change. I thought that it could be utilized to teach empathy. I eventually came to the conclusion that I was dead wrong. Sentimentality and empathy were totally different!
- The criminal shuts off sentiment just like someone flips off a light switch. Sentiment and savage brutality reside side by side in the same individual. One has no bearing on the other.

The Criminal's Thinking in Extremes

He is number one or else a "nothing"
Published on October 5, 2012 by Stanton E. Samenow, Ph.D. in Inside the Criminal Mind

The criminal does not know what moderation is! In his thinking and behavior, he more frequently than not goes to extremes. It is critical to understand this aspect of his psychological makeup. Failure to do so can endanger a person who interviews, attempts to counsel, or in other ways interacts with a criminal.

In his mind, the criminal must be number one or else he counts for nothing — an intolerable situation. You can see this even when he is a child. If others don't play by his rules, he refuses to play at all. If he is not recognized as tops in any endeavor that matters to him — e.g., sports, academics — then it isn't worth doing. Even in a menial task in prison such as buffing a floor, it must shine. If someone steps on it before he has completed the job, he becomes furious. He is indiscriminant in this view that everything he does must be tops and recognized as such by others. Everything has the same importance. This is not a quest for excellence but a result of his own pretensions.

The criminal demands that others recognize him as "number one" when it comes to work. If he walks into a restaurant seeking a job, he believes that he should be the manager, not a "lackey" who has to undertake tasks that he regards as beneath him.

In even the smallest interactions, the criminal is determined to prevail. Thus, he does not know what a discussion involves. He is insistent on proving his point, not exchanging views. Only what he thinks and says matters. Others disagreeing with him he interprets as threatening, even on a trivial point.

People are either for him or against him. There are no in-betweens. If you don't go along with what he wants, support his position, agree with what he is saying, he will ignore you, try to verbally beat you down or, at worst, attack you physically.

Clearly, this black and white view of the world leads to a criminal's expectations being constantly thwarted. Constantly, he is perceiving that he has been putdown or diminished by others even when no offense is intended. This is a factor in the constant anger that the criminal experiences because he frequently does not receive the response from others that he desires and believes he is due.

Inside the Criminal Mind

Understanding the dark side of human conduct.
by Dr. Stanton E. Samenow, Ph.D.

The Male Criminal's Choice of Women

The ultimate "male chauvinist"
Published on August 17, 2012 by Stanton E. Samenow, Ph.D. in Inside the Criminal Mind

The ultimate male chauvinist is the person with a criminal personality. Inasmuch as the world revolves around him, or so he believes, a woman is to do his bidding. He is to have his wishes met. He is not to be challenged. In fact, he may refer to a female as "his" woman as though she is a possession. And he treats her as such.

Actually, there are two patterns. Some criminals find women who are very much like themselves— excitement seekers and controllers. As one man said, "Us kinds find each other." These relationships are unstable and often explosive as each struggles to control the other. The relationships usually are short-lived. Each partner uses the other for sex, money, and whatever else he or she wants. Domestic violence is common. If such a duo has children, the offspring are often neglected or mistreated; if not physically, then emotionally. If a divorce occurs with a custody battle, the tactics are ferocious by which each seeks to gain the upper hand. Child custody is like a trophy. Winning matters more than the welfare of the child.

The second, and probably more common, pattern is the criminal finding a female who is insecure and emotionally needy. Such a woman may be swept off her feet, so to speak, by a man who is charismatic, charming, and exciting. In short order, her world revolves him. Linda came from a small town and had had little experience with men. She met and quickly fell in love with Douglas. She was captivated by his gregarious personality and his good looks. He showered her with gifts and took her on excursions. One day, he picked her up and surprised her by transporting her to a beautiful wooded area for a camping expedition and a picnic. Linda knew that Douglas worked at a job that didn't pay much, but he had extremely expensive camping equipment. When she asked him about how he afforded this gear, he laughed off her question, then with an edge said, "Don't ask anything you don't want the answer to." She ceased questioning the things that he said or did. One day, Linda received a phone call informing her that Douglas had been arrested for shoplifting. She thought it was her fault, that if she had been kinder and more affectionate, he never would have done such a thing. The two continued to date. Every minute of her existence that she was not working was given over to her paramour. She was intent on never disappointing Douglas and did whatever he asked.

The more Linda got to know Douglas, the more she discovered how irritable he became if she disagreed with him over even a seemingly trivial matter. More than once, she thought maybe she should start dating others. But she had little confidence in herself, and he had convinced her that no one could ever love her as much as he did. After months of an increasingly rocky relationship, Linda received another call. Douglas had been arrested for rape. Still Linda believed that it must have been something that she had done or failed to do that "caused" her boyfriend to do what he did. Certain she could do no better, she vowed to wait for him, no matter how long he was in jail.

It is typical for a criminal like Douglas to capitalize on the lack of self-confidence of women who develop a strong and unhealthy psychological and financial dependence. Most important to their remaining steadfastly loyal is their belief that they could do no better. Furthermore, it becomes increasingly difficult and, in some cases, dangerous to try to leave such a relationship. These women continue to live in abusive relationships, often blaming themselves for what goes awry.

Inside the Criminal Mind

Understanding the dark side of human conduct.
by Dr. Stanton E. Samenow, Ph.D.

Armed Robber and Corporate Crook: Similar Mentalities

Only the modus operandi differs; thought patterns are the same
Published on July 7, 2012 by Stanton E. Samenow, Ph.D. in Inside the Criminal Mind

Despite possible differences in educational and socio-economic background and an obvious difference in the manner in which they execute their crimes, the mentality of a person who robs a bank and a corporate executive who perpetrates fraud is the same. Both pursue power and control at the expense of others. Both are able to shut off considerations of consequences and conscience long enough to do what they want. Neither has an operational concept of injury to others. Neither puts himself/herself in the place of others.

The offense for which either offender is caught, more likely than not, represents just the tip of the iceberg of each offender's irresponsibility and illegal conduct. Both know right from wrong, but whatever they are doing at the time is "right" to their way of thinking. They know the laws and calculate carefully so they can succeed at their objective. The robber and "white collar" offender both conceive of themselves as totally unique and smarter than others. They experience a certain excitement during each phase of the crime — from the initial idea through the execution of the act and its aftermath. If apprehended, each will case out those who hold them accountable and feed them what they think they want to hear or ought to know. And they will do their utmost to dispel responsibility by implicating or blaming others.

Inside the Criminal Mind

Understanding the dark side of human conduct.
by Dr. Stanton E. Samenow, Ph.D.

Typing Offenders by Crime—Concealing More than Revealing?

Typing offenders by crime rarely helps understanding who the offender is.
Published on November 16, 2011 by Stanton E. Samenow, Ph.D. in Inside the Criminal Mind

When a man is arrested and convicted of rape, he is known as a rapist and a sex offender. When an individual is convicted of distributing narcotics, he is known as a drug dealer. However, what a person is arrested for constitutes, in most instances, the tip of the iceberg. In more than 40 years of interviewing offenders, every rapist whom I have interviewed has committed crimes other than rape — e.g., nonsexual assaults, theft. Even typing a person as a "white collar" offender may not be accurate. I have interviewed white-collar individuals who have committed acts of domestic violence, alcohol abuse, and drug abuse.

It is true that offenders have tastes and preferences in crime. The white-collar offender looks down on the violent street criminal as crude and as sharing nothing in common with him. The guy who resorts to force ("muscle") may look down on someone not so inclined as "sissy," "lame," or "weak."

The key to understanding the psychological makeup of offenders is not so much the type of crime that they are known for, but the thinking processes that all offenders share in common, no matter what criminal activity they engage in.

Power and control, shutting off deterrents from conscious thought, the view of the self as unique, the lack of a concept of injury to others — these and many other thinking patterns are evidenced by offenders who, otherwise, appear to be very different from one another.

In short, the crime for which a person is arrested represents only the tip of an iceberg of irresponsibility and criminality that, in more cases than not, has yet come to light.

SOURCE: PSYCHOLOGY TODAY

So hopefully now you have a clearer understanding of the criminal mind. Seeing how warped and pathetic they are could lead one to actually feel sorry for them. Don't! Don't get suckered in by their charms or sob stories! I always tell young ladies especially, go by what they do, not what they say. Action speaks louder than words.

Finally, I know that all of this information is disheartening and somewhat disturbing, but remember; no matter how bad things seem, there are more of us (good guys), than there are of them (bad guys). We can and will always prevail.

SECTION XVI – WEAPONS OF CHOICE

" . . . Weapons are important but not decisive. It is a man's directing intelligence which counts most"

—MAO TSE-TUNG

Now that you know what you're up against, you may decide to arm yourself to aid in your self-defense efforts. Many people don't like the idea using weapons to harm another human being, but it may become necessary when they find themselves on the wrong end of a Criminal's violent act. If you've never faced a Violent Criminal or been a victim of violent crime, then yes, the concept of arming yourself for protection may not be so appealing. But for those us who have been through the fire; we know that it is both wise and necessary to bring an equalizer to fight! Besides, there is no such thing as a fair fight. We cheat to win! Your goal is to win at all costs! Remember; the Criminal has no qualms about arming himself and using that weapon against you to get what he wants.

It is important that you know what type weapon suits you best or the situation that you are in. If the situation permits, do some research on your weapon(s) of choice. Let's look at your options:

1. **Pepper Spray/Mace**—My personal favorite. It is easy to acquire, easy to use, and it does not cause permanent damage.
2. **Stun Gun**—Electronic Weapon that requires direct contact to the human body to cause pain. They are very painful but do not cause permanent damage. There are some that come disguised as a small Flashlight or a Cane and delivers a one million volt shock.
3. **Taser**—Electronic Weapon that deploys prongs into the human body and delivers a 50,000 volt shock that shuts down the body's muscular system. It can also be used as a Stun Gun by bringing it into contact with the human body. It is a very effective non-lethal weapon.
4. **Impact Weapons**—The ASP Baton is an example of defensive impact weapon. It is collapsible and easy to use. It comes in several different sizes and like the Taser, is used by Law Enforcement Agencies. The Kubaton a very small, but very effective impact device that can be easily concealed.
5. **Firearms**—There are many types of handguns, shotguns, and rifles available to you for self-defense. Go to a trained, qualified, and licensed source such as a Gun Store or Gun Range for advice on firearms. Try out several types of firearms before you buy. Then, take the appropriate training courses to familiarize yourself with

the weapon further and get your concealed carry permit. Firearms are always at the Deadly Force level.

6. **Improvised Weapons**—Anything that isn't nailed down that can be used to hit the aggressor with. That includes ink pens, frying pans, vehicles, apples, bug spray, and chairs. [See any of the Jason Bourne movies]. Just be sure that you are using the appropriate level of force when improvising.

Listed here are the laws for concealed weapon carry and use in Florida. The laws may be different where you live.

CARRYING CONCEALED WEAPONS.—

(1) Except as provided in subsection (4), a person who carries a concealed weapon or electric weapon or device on or about his or her person commits a misdemeanor of the first degree, punishable as provided in s. 775.082 or s. 775.083.

(2) A person who carries a concealed firearm on or about his or her person commits a felony of the third degree, punishable as provided in s. 775.082, s. 775.083, or s. 775.084.

(3) This section does not apply to a person licensed to carry a concealed weapon or a concealed firearm pursuant to the provisions of s. 790.06.

(4) It is not a violation of this section for a person to carry for purposes of lawful self-defense, in a concealed manner:
  (a) A self-defense chemical spray.
  (b) A nonlethal stun gun or dart-firing stun gun or other nonlethal electric weapon or device that is designed solely for defensive purposes.

(5) This section does not preclude any prosecution for the use of an electric weapon or device, a dart-firing stun gun, or a self-defense chemical spray during the commission of any criminal offense under s. 790.07, s. 790.10, s. 790.23, or s. 790.235, or for any other criminal offense.

2. **790.053 f.s.** **Abstract:** —(1) Except as otherwise provided by law and in subsection (2), it is unlawful for any person to openly carry on or about his or her person any firearm or electric weapon or device. 790.06(1), and who is lawfully carrying a firearm in a concealed manner, to briefly and openly display the firearm to the ordinary sight of another person, unless the firearm is intentionally displayed in an angry or threatening manner, not in necessary self-defense. (2) A person may openly . . .

3. **790.01 f.s.** **Abstract:** —(1) Except as provided in subsection (4), a person who carries a concealed weapon or electric weapon or device on or about his or her person commits a misdemeanor of the first degree, punishable as provided in s. (3) This section does not apply to a person licensed to carry a concealed weapon or a concealed firearm pursuant to the provisions of s. (4) It is not a violation of this section for a person to carry for purposes of lawful self-defense, in a concealed . . .

4. **790.251 f.s.** **Abstract:** —No public or private employer may violate the constitutional rights of any customer, employee, or invitee as provided in paragraphs (a)-(e):(a) No public or private employer may prohibit any customer, employee, or invitee from possessing any legally owned firearm when such firearm is lawfully possessed and locked inside or locked to a private motor vehicle in a parking lot and when the customer, employee, or invitee is lawfully in such area. (f) A motor vehicle owned, . . .

790.054 f.s. **Abstract:** 790.054 Prohibited use of self-defense weapon or device against law enforcement officer; penalties. —A person who knowingly and willfully uses a self-defense chemical spray, a nonlethal stun gun or other nonlethal electric weapon or device, or a dart-firing stun gun against a law enforcement officer engaged in the performance of his or her duties commits a felony of the third degree, punishable as provided in s. 775.083, or s.

6. **790.001 f.s.** **Abstract:** (3)(a) "Concealed weapon" means any dirk, metallic knuckles, slungshot, billie, tear gas gun, chemical weapon or device, or other deadly weapon carried on or about a person in such a manner as to conceal the weapon from the ordinary sight of another person. (b) "Tear gas gun" or "chemical weapon or device" means any weapon of such nature, except a device known as a "self-defense chemical spray. (13) "Weapon" means any dirk, knife, metallic knuckles, slungshot, billie, . . .

SOURCE: FLORIDA STATE STATUES

SECTION XVII – ACTIVE COUNTERMEASURES!

"Malice is ever alert, and much thought is necessary to outwit her, a gambler does not play the card which his opponent expects much less that which he desires"

-BALTASAR GRACIAN

The Aphorism above was written in the 16th Century, and of course nothing about human nature has really changed. Criminals are constantly and relentlessly searching for ways to wreak havoc on the law-abiding and unsuspecting members of our society! Plainly said; you must always be on your toes to outwit the ever-present threat to your personal safety and should you find yourself face to face with evil, always use the element of surprise to achieve victory! In other words; ***CHEAT TO WIN!***

Years ago the term Active Countermeasures was used by Law Enforcement to describe Defensive Tactics, or using physical force to overcome criminal aggression. We are going to take that same terminology and use it to describe the steps to you will take to actively engage an immediate threat against your personal safety or life.

The OODA LOOP

Studies have shown that there are four stages that the brain goes through when confronted with danger or an unfamiliar situation. This concept is widely used to train Military and Law Enforcement personnel on the process they (or the criminal), go through when placed in dynamic situations. The process is called the **OODA** Loop.

1. **Observe**—You observe an event unfolding in front of you.
2. **Orient**—Your mind orients to the event and decides that it is a threat.
3. **Decide**—You decide on a plan of action to escape, counter, or subdue the threat.
4. **Act**—You take decisive action.

Soldiers, Police Officers, Athletes, and even Criminals go through the OODA Loop much faster than the average person by virtue of training and/or experience. You must find your **Inner Warrior** and get through this process faster so that you can increase your odds in the face of mortal danger. To do this, you must train regularly. Practice the techniques that you have learned so far. Learn to use visualization drills to help prepare your mind for the unthinkable.

Find some quiet time during your day to imagine a dangerous scenario such as an Active Shooter attack, a Home Invasion, a Physical Attack by a stranger, or a Domestic Violence situation. See yourself responding in a way that you are victorious!! See yourself winning!

HOME—Is your home defense up to speed? Do you have an alarm? If so, do you use it? If you have a home alarm, you should use it even when you're home. Most of the newer apartments have alarm systems. If yours doesn't, you can purchase inexpensive wireless alarm system from a variety of sources. I recommend that all doors and windows should be alarmed. There are all kinds of inexpensive and effective tools out there to secure your home. There are even door handles that you can install that have alarms built into them.

Make sure that trees and shrubs don't grow so high that criminals can easily hide behind them. The standard CPTED rule, (Crime Prevention Through Environmental Design), is to trim trees six feet up, and shrubs down to no higher than three feet. Use good lighting around the exterior of your home. Don't give criminals darkness to hide in.

Lock your bedroom door when you go to bed at night (particularly if you are a woman that lives alone).

If you choose to use a weapon as part of your home defense, make sure that you can access that weapon at all times, particularly if you are in a high-threat situation.

Do you have a home defense plan? Have you trained your children on what to do should the unthinkable happens? Have you done a dry run of your home defense plans?

Do you know what to do if you come home during a Burglary to your home? Most times when people arrive home and find an open door or broken window, they go into the house (just like in the movies), look around, and then call the police. Often times the Burglar is still inside!

Active Countermeasures thinking dictates a different response. You come home and find a door open, a window broken, or a strange vehicle backed into your driveway. Don't take chances; leave the scene and call the police immediately from a safe distance! Do not engage the bad guys and don't play detective!

Do you and your family members know what to do if a Burglar breaks in while you/they are home? Recently, a friend's daughter (22 years old), was home alone when a Burglar attempted to break into their apartment by coming through the ceiling. The Burglar had broken into the vacant apartment next door, climbed up into the attic, and crawled over to the victim's apartment. The young lady saw the man's feet come through the ceiling and panicked. Remember **Colonel Cooper's Color Code Awareness System**? The young lady's mind went into the **Black** mode. Instead of dialing 911 and getting immediate help **(Immediate Action Drills)**, she froze. She didn't run and hide or flee the scene. She simply stood there and watched in disbelief! Luckily, the bad guy realized that someone was home and retreated back the way he came. Even then the young lady failed to act properly and called her mother, not the police. This was a classic example a victim making all of the wrong decisions.

Again, **Active Countermeasures** thinking dictates a different response. The young lady should have immediately dialed 911, then, either barricaded in a different room or fled the apartment. Had she been armed she could have used force to defend herself and her home.

DRIVING—Okay, you're driving along and you accidentally (or purposely), cut someone off and they come after you. I have listened to numerous calls like this and the victim drives around mindlessly while the aggressor gets more agitated and keeps the police running around trying to find them. Know your city! Get the location of the police station or stations in your city and lock the address into your GPS (if you have one). Do not stop until the police arrive! Don't count on bystanders to save you! Honk your horn! Turn on your emergency flashers! If you have a personal defense device (weapon) in your vehicle, get it ready to use. Don't let the aggressor approach your vehicle! Do not get out of your vehicle until the police arrive! Remain calm!

AT WORK—This one is fairly simple. Take notice when one of your co-workers is acting or talking dangerously suspicious. Alert the company management, security and/or the police. Take notice if they are having serious domestic problems. If you are aware of such issues, always check the parking lot/garage when you arrive and leave. Don't be caught unprepared! Read up on Active Shooter situations. There is plenty of information out there on what to do. Your company should have some type of training. There's a video on the Internet out called Run, Fight, Hide! Get it and watch it with your co-workers and/or family. Listen, when you see a potentially dangerous event happening in front of you, you are not watching a movie! It is real life and it is happening to you right then and there! Move to a safe location, dial 911 if necessary! Also, because the potential for gun violence; teach your kids not to stand around and watch fights at school or around the neighborhood.

IN PUBLIC—As you know, almost anything goes in our society these days. Always be on guard when you are out among your fellow human beings. Stay in **Code Yellow** at all times. Someone once asked me what I have learned about people in all my years in Law Enforcement. I told her two things:

1. **People are not nearly as good as they pretend to be.**
2. **People are not nearly as smart as think they are**.

So that means that you are out among people who are not so nice and not too bright! Now add some real criminals into the mix and you have yourself a real party!! So stay on your toes and be aware! (Unfortunately, this cannot be taught, awareness must be developed . . .).

Do not let strangers get too close to you. (For example, Panhandlers, People asking for directions, etc . . .).

When using the ATM, don't get too engrossed in the transaction. Look around every few seconds. Do not use the ATM at night if it is in an isolated area!!

HIGH THREAT SITUATIONS—If someone is threatening you, don't wait until the attack to make your move. Prep your defensive measures, (weapons, dial 911, etc . . .). Strike first, strike fast, strike hard!

Criminals often (but not always), put a lot of preparation into their crimes. The preparation is usually on the "how violent can I be during this crime", scale. So as I said earlier; the criminal has his/her engine already revved up! You, the good citizen will have to play catch up in the middle of a violent attack!

Basically**, Active Countermeasures** is seeing the threat as it emerges and taking aggressive and positive action to save yourself and/or others. Of course, the goal is always to win! If winning means escaping, evading, or surviving, then that is what you should do! Taking proper and effective action is critical to winning. Get some professional training; and then practice often. Your reaction must be instinctive, fluid, and calm. Always remember to be **C**ool **U**nder **P**ressure. This is the key to winning.

FIRST AID TRAINING—Learn basic CPR and basic First Aid techniques such as how to treat minor wounds, broken bones, or shock. There are numerous books and manuals on the subject of First Aid.

RESCUE BREATHING—It is important to remain calm when faced with life-threatening events. Rescue Breathing can help keep you calm and focused and save your life. Practice this at home when you have some time alone:

Breathe in for four counts, hold your breath for four counts, breathe out for four counts, hold your breath for four counts. Breathe in through your nose, out through your mouth. Repeat this drill until you are calm. A **variation** of this drill is to breathe deeply in through the nose, and forcefully out through the mouth without the four count.

UNARMED COMBAT TRAINING—The following is an excerpt taken from a book on Special Forces training: Taking up a martial art can assist with the speed, power, and reflexes required to perform well in the SAS's Close Quarter Battle unarmed combat training.

There are a huge variety of martial arts to choose from, and not all are appropriate. Choose a 'hard' art—training which emphasizes the overcoming of an opponent by force and power (karate, kickboxing, kung fu, etc.,)—rather than a 'soft' art such as Aikido which concentrates on blending with the attack and repelling by generally non-damaging throws and pushes. Good martial arts to try specifically for SAS preparation are Ju Jitsu, Karate (particularly a close quarter form such as Goju Ru), kickboxing and hard styles of kung fu.

Alternatively, join a reputable self-defence class which teaches realistic self-defence-remember that delicate wristlocks will not work on highly aggressive and non-compliant opponents set on killing you. SAS CQB trains in a very few effective and straightforward techniques—it is not a martial art but some prior preparation will help your body respond quickly to the training.

Chris McNab
THE SAS TRAINING MANUAL

This insert was added for your review and consideration. It is a good and accurate offering and is basically the same information that I give to police officers when they ask me about martial arts or self-defense training. USA GOJU, Kyokushin Karate, and several other "hard' styles are the basis of my self-defense platform. You must find what works for you.

***Note*The SAS (Special Air Service), is the British Special Forces.**

FIREARMS TRAINING—Should you decide to use a firearm for personal defense, get professional training. Learn how to properly handle firearms and how to use them to defend yourself, your family, or other law-abiding citizens. Be sure to adhere to the laws where you live and get the proper licensing for weapons carry/ownership.

This concludes your Level One training. Practice, study, and be prepared.